M000003020

MAJOR & MRS HOLT'S
POCKET BATTLEFIELD GUIDE TO

YPRES &
PASSCHENDAELE

First Battle of Ypres: 18 October – 11 November 1914
Second Battle of Ypres (Gas Attack): 22 April – 25 May 1915
Third Battle of Ypres (Passchendaele): 7 June – 10 November 1917

Ploegsteert Memorial

MAJOR & MRS HOLT'S
POCKET BATTLEFIELD GUIDE TO

YPRES &
PASSCHENDAELE

Tonie & Valmai Holt

By the same authors
Picture Postcards of the Golden Age: A Collector's Guide
Till the Boys Come Home: the Picture Postcards of the First World War
The Best of Fragments from France by Capt Bruce Bairnsfather,
revised Edition for 'Help For Heroes', 2009
In Search of the Better 'Ole: The Life, Works and Collectables of Bruce Bairnsfather,
revised edition 2001 Picture Postcard Artists: Landscapes, Animals and Characters
Stanley Gibbons Postcard Catalogue: 1980, 1981, 1982, 1984, 1985, 1987
Germany Awake! The Rise of National Socialism illustrated by Contemporary Postcards
I'll be Seeing You: the Picture Postcards of World War II
Violets From Oversea: Reprinted as Poets of the Great War, 1999, 2004, 2010
My Boy Jack?: The Search for Kipling's Only Son: revised limpback editions 2008, 2009, 2010
Holts' Battlefield Guidebooks: Normandy-Overlord/Market-Garden/Somme/Ypres
Visitor's Guide to the Normandy Landing Beaches
Battlefields of the First World War: A Traveller's Guide
Major & Mrs Holt's Concise Guide to the Ypres Salient
Major & Mrs Holt's Battle Maps: Normandy/Somme/Ypres-Passchendaele/Gallipoli/MARKET-GARDEN
Major & Mrs Holt's Battlefield Guide to the Ypres Salient + Battle Map
Major & Mrs Holt's Battlefield Guide to The Somme + Battle Map
Major & Mrs Holt's Battlefield Guide to Gallipoli + Battle Map
Major & Mrs Holt's Battlefield Guide to MARKET-GARDEN (Arnhem) + Battle Map
Major & Mrs Holt's Battlefield Guide to Normandy D-Day Landing Beaches + Battle Map
The Definitive Battlefield Guide to the Normandy D-Day Landing Beaches by Major & Mrs Holt
Major & Mrs Holt's Concise, Illustrated Battlefield Guide to the Western Front – North
Major & Mrs Holt's Concise, Illustrated Battlefield Guide to the Western Front – South
Major & Mrs Holt's Pocket Battlefield Guide to the Somme
Major & Mrs Holt's Pocket Battlefield Guide to the Normandy Landing Beaches/D-Day

First published in Great Britain in 2006, this third revised edition 2011 by
Pen & Sword MILITARY
an imprint of
Pen & Sword Books Limited
47 Church Street, Barnsley, South Yorkshire, S70 2AS

Text copyright © Tonie and Valmai Holt, 2011
Except where otherwise credited, all illustrations remain the copyright of Tonie and Valmai Holt.
The moral rights of the authors have been asserted.

ISBN: 1 84415 377 0
ISBN: 978 1 84415 377 0

*The rights of Tonie and Valmai Holt to be identified as Authors of this Work have been asserted by
them in accordance with the Copyright, Designs and Patents Act 1988. A CIP catalogue record for this
book is available from the British Library.*

All rights reserved. No part of this book may be reproduced or transmitted in any form or by any
means, electronic or mechanical including photocopying, recording or by any information storage and
retrieval system, without permission from the Publisher in writing.

Typeset in 8.5pt Optima by Pen & Sword Books Limited
Printed and bound in India by Replika Press Pvt. Ltd.

For a complete list of Pen & Sword titles please contact
Pen & Sword Books Ltd, 47 Church St, Barnsley, S. Yorkshire, S70 2AS, England
email: enquiries@pen-and-sword.co.uk
website: www.pen-and-sword.co.uk

CONTENTS

Introduction

The Dead

These hearts were woven of human joys and cares,
Washed marvellously with sorrow, swift to mirth.
The years had given them kindness. Dawn was theirs,
And sunset, and the colours of the earth.
These had seen movement, and heard music; Known
　　slumber and waking; loved; gone proudly friended;
Felt the quick stir of wonder; sat alone;
Touched flowers and furs and cheeks. All this is ended.
Rupert Brooke. Sonnet No IV. 1914

*Sub-Lt Rupert Brooke, RN
died 23 April 1915.*
Portrait by Charlotte Zeepva

This 'Pocket' Guide to Ypres and Passchendaele is designed for those who have limited time to visit this historic and emotive battlefield. Suggestions for the best use of a day or half a day are given below and those who have more time at their disposal and/or a deeper interest in the Battles of Ypres should refer to our **Major & Mrs Holt's Battlefield Guide to the Ypres Salient & Passchendaele**. Those who would like to put the Ypres Battles in their chronological and historical context are directed towards our **Major & Mrs Holt's Concise, Illustrated Guide to the Western Front – North.**

Throughout the Great War of 1914-1918 only one corner of Belgium remained unconquered. In this rough, half-moon shape known as 'The Salient', an eternal bond between the Belgian and British nations was formed. To this day that bond is movingly renewed every evening at 2000 hours when, under Sir Reginald Blomfield's impressive Menin Gate Memorial, buglers from Ypres sound the Last Post in memory of their British and Commonwealth Allies.

During four years of fighting for a few kilometres of land an average of 5,000 British and Commonwealth soldiers died every month. By 1918 almost one million had been wounded. The ground was flat, the weather frequently wet and the trenches readily filled with water. Added to the dangers of cannon and machine guns were the Salient inventions of the *Flammenwer*fer and poison gas. To die there was easy. 'Wipers' and 'Passchendaele' were names that became engraved on the hearts of many Australian, British, Canadian and Indian family hearts, for the men of the Dominions had rallied early and enthusiastically to the cause of the Mother Country.

There were many famous names who fought and died in the Salient, like Prince Maurice of Battenberg, the poets Julian Grenfell, Francis Ledwidge and 'Hedd Wynn' (Pte Ellis Humphrey Evans) and the VCs Capt Noel Chavasse, Capt Francis Grenfell and Brig Gen Charles FitzClarence, as well as the inspiration for Bruce Bairnsfather's immortal Old Bill, L/Cpl 'Pat' Rafferty, who is commemorated on the Menin Gate. It was, however, the common soldier who carried the heaviest burden as the terrifyingly vast list of names on the Menin Gate, the Tyne Cot Memorial and the New Zealand Memorials at Polygon Wood and on the Messines Ridge bear witness. There are almost 55,000 names on the Menin Gate and nearly 35,000 at Tyne Cot. None have known graves.

The Ypres Salient is an area whose fascination continues to

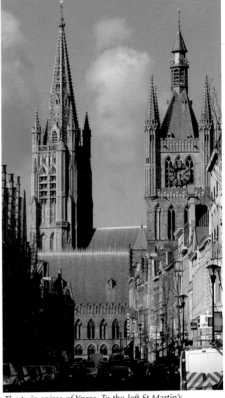

The twin spires of Ypres. To the left St Martin's Cathedral. To the right the Belfry tower, Cloth Hall.

exert a hold even as we approach the Centenary of the outbreak of the Great War in August 1914 and the ensuing four years of 100th Anniversaries. Major projects are planned for the 'In Flanders Fields Museum', the Passchendaele Memorial Museum, the Information Centre at Lissjenthoek, Bayernwald Trenches and many other sites in the Salient that may disrupt normal visiting over the next few years. Now that the last veteran of WW1, Harry Patch (qv), is no longer with us to pass his memories on, the land itself has truly become 'The Last Witness' and the Westhoek Tourist authorities with their *War and Peace in the Westhoek* are making sure that the land is a truly eloquent and lasting witness.

Since we conducted our first tour in 1977, when no other post-WW2 organised tours existed for the general public, the battlefield scene has changed beyond all recognition. Then we would stand alone with the faithful buglers at the Menin Gate, be the sole signatories in remote cemetery registers, place our poppy tributes on rarely visited memorials. It was a very privileged time. Gradually the interest and momentum rolled on. Local authorities realised that battlefields could equate to tourism. Designated routes were devised and signed, sites were refurbished, made safe for visitors, car parks were constructed, small museums with superb personal exhibits but little professional curatorship skills were expanded and 'modernised'. Perhaps a little of the 'soul' was lost in the process but now, as battlefield touring has moved from the exclusive realms of the 'buff ' or the 'pilgrim' to that of the 'student' and the 'tourist', the benefit is that so many more people are able to be exposed to the lore of the Great War and can contribute to keeping the memory alive.

The ever-continuing research by armchair historians and energetic local enthusiasts alike has led to a flood of new information and the discovery and opening up of new sites to visit. In the Ypres Salient 'The Diggers' (qv) discovered the treasures under the developing industrial estate at Boezinge; one of the great craters has been opened to visits at St Eloi; the fascinating Canal Bank site at Essex Farm has been exploited; Talbot House in Poperinge has opened a Visitor Centre in the old adjacent Hop Store; Zonnebeke has completely remodelled its Museum and opened up the historical remains at Bayernwald; interesting tunnel entrances have been refurbished on the Letterberg at Kemmel; new Interpretative Centres and parking facilities have been created behind Tyne Cot Cemetery and at Langemarck German Cemetery. The expansion seems never ending.

What is important is to keep alight the flame thrown to our hands by John McCrae in the best-known poem of the Great War: *In Flanders Fields*. In writing this book – the fulfilment of almost 40 years of studying and visiting the battlefields – we have endeavoured to hold it high and now pass it to you. The Rupert Brooke poem, one of his collection of *Sonnets*, published in 1915 and reproduced at the beginning of this Introduction, has many resonances of the McCrae poem, also published in 1915. Both poems highlight the tragedy of lost youth that we still mourn today.

Tonie and Valmai Holt,
Woodnesborough, 2010

About the Authors

Respected military authors Tonie and Valmai Holt are acknowledged as the founders, in the 1970s, of the modern battlefield tour. Valmai Holt took a BA(Hons) in French and Spanish and taught History. Tonie Holt took a BSc(Eng) and is a graduate of the Royal Military Academy, Sandhurst and of the Army Staff College at Camberley. They are both Fellows of the Royal Society of Arts and Science and have made frequent appearances on the lecture circuit, radio and television. They are founder members of The Western Front Association and Honorary Members of the Guild of Battlefield Guides.

Their company, *Major & Mrs Holt's Battlefield Tours,* organised tours for Purnell & BCA Book Clubs, covering the American Civil War, Arnhem, the Crimea, El Alamein, Monte Cassino, the Normandy Landing Beaches, Vietnam, Waterloo, the WW1 Gallipoli, Italian and Western Fronts, the Falkland Islands, South Africa and many other destinations.

In the 1980s they took over the organisation of the RBL Pilgrimages and acted as consultants to the cities of Portsmouth and Southampton, The *Département* of Calvados, Townsend Thoresen and British Airways for the 40th Anniversary, of the D-Day Landings and were appointed ADCs to Congressman Robert Livingston of Louisiana for services in support of American veterans.

Their *Major & Mrs Holt's Battlefield Guides* series comprises, without doubt, the leading guide books to the battlefields of the First and Second World Wars. Their unique combination of male and female viewpoints allows military commentaries to be linked with the poetry, music and literature of the period under study and can draw upon over 30 years experience gained in personally conducting thousands of people around the areas they have written about. In the early days they were privileged to be able to record the memories of veterans of the Great War and then WW2, which have been incorporated into their books.

In December 2003 the Holts sponsored a memorial to Capt Bruce Bairnsfather (the subject of their biography, *In Search of the Better 'Ole*) at St Yvon near 'Plugstreet' Wood' and in 2009, the 50th Anniversary year of the death of the cartoonist Bruce Bairnsfather, they updated their 1978 published collection of 140 of his most enduring cartoons, T*he Best of Fragments from France.* This, together with tribute cartoons donated by some of the world's leading cartoonists and sold at a Charity Auction, raised well over £7,000.00 for 'Help for Heroes'. All authors' royalties from the sale of the book also go to the Charity.

*For more information and latest news **VISIT THEIR WEBSITE**:*
www.guide-books.co.uk

Abbreviations

Abbreviations and acronyms used for military units are listed below. Many of these are printed in full at intervals throughout the text to aid clarity. Others are explained where they occur.

A/	Acting	MM	Military Medal
ADS	Advanced Dressing Station	OP	Observation Point
AIF	Australian Imperial Force	OR	Other Rank(s)
Arty	Artillery	ORBAT	Order of Battle
Att/d	Attached	POW's	Prince of Wales/Prisoners of War
Aust	Australian		
Bde	Brigade	Pte	Private
BEF	British Expeditionary Force	RF	Royal Fusiliers
Bn	Battalion	RE	Royal Engineers
Brit	British	RFA	Royal Field Artillery
Can	Canadian	RIF	Royal Inniskilling Fusiliers
C-in-C	Commander-in-Chief	RWF	Royal Welsh Fusiliers
CO	Commanding Officer	SGW	Stained Glass Window
Comm	Communal	T/	Temporary
Coy	Company	VC	Victoria Cross
CWGC	Commonwealth War Graves Commission	WFA	Western Front Association
Div	Division		
Ger	German		
GHQ	General Head Quarters		
Gnr	Gunner		
HAC	Honorable Artillery Company		
HLI	Highland Light Infantry		
Inf	Infantry		
IWGC	Imperial War Graves Commission		
KOYLI	King's Own Yorkshire Light Infantry		
KRRC	King's Royal Rifle Corps		
L/	Lance		
Mia	Missing in action		
MC	Military Cross		

The Holts checking out the Ypres map.

How to use this Guide

This book may be read at home as a continuous account, used en-route as a guide to specific actions and places, dipped into at any time via the Index as a source of fascinating detail about the Ypres Salient or kept as a reminder of past visits to the sites described.

Each battle is separately described under the headings 'A Summary of the Battle', 'Opening Moves' and 'What Happened' to remind readers of its historical significance, so that the details may be more readily understood and to provide a framework upon which the accounts that follow may be hung. Each battle described is accompanied by an especially drawn map and the conduct of the battles can be more easily followed by constant references to the appropriate map.

At the front of each chapter are one or more quotations from people who were involved in the war and these have been chosen to give a relevant, sometimes provocative, personal flavour to the detailed accounts. Those already familiar with the First World War will find the chapter quotations apposite before reading further, while those less familiar may well find it worthwhile to read the quotations again at a later stage.

Latitude and Longitude References

These have been added to all major stops on the Battlefield Tour for this edition, enabling the readers who wish to go directly to specific sites to do so using their 'satnavs'. The references refer to the closest parking place to the site. Though a satellite navigation system can be a great help, we do not recommend that you rely exclusively upon it as it may direct you away from a route that is integral to an understanding of the 'shape' of a battle.

Making a Short Visit: Two Suggested Itineraries

The full battlefield tour set out later in this book would be best done over two days. These two itineraries immediately below are for those who do not have that amount of time.

Directions for, and descriptions of, these highlights are found by consulting the page references given.

1. If you have one long day available:
(assuming early and late ferry or tunnel crossings from and to the UK or an early start if already in Belgium)

Talbot House, Poperinge (page 36)
In Flanders Fields Museum (page 41)
St George's Memorial Church (page 43)
Essex Farm (page 46)
German Cemetery & Interpretative Centre, Langemarck (page 50)
Vancouver Corner (page 52)
Tyne Cot Cemetery & Interpretative Centre (page 55)
Passchendaele Museum, Zonnebeke (page 58)
Sanctuary Wood (page 69)
Last Post, Menin Gate 2000 hours (page 44, 94)

2. If you have half a day:

In Flanders Fields Museum (page 41)
Menin Gate (pages 44, 94)
Essex Farm (page 46)
Vancouver Corner (page 52)
Tyne Cot Cemetery & Interpretative Centre (page 55)

Miles Covered/Duration/OP/RWC/ Travel Directions/Extra Visits/'N.B.s'

The battlefield tours that we suggest cover features that during our many years of guiding parties across, and writing about, the battlefields, have been the most requested as being the best-known, the most important, the most emotive... Added to them are the new sites that have recently been opened up. None is exhaustive – this is a '*Pocket*' battlefield guide – but in combination with the specially drawn maps for each battle they provide a compact and hopefully illuminating commentary upon the events of the time, from glimpses of the 'Grand Designs', through individual acts of heroism to the memorials that now mark the pride and grief of a past generation.

A start point is given for each tour from which a running total of miles is indicated. Extra visits are not counted in that running total. Each recommended stop is indicated by a clear heading with the running total, the probable time you will wish to stay there and a map reference to the relevant Sketch Map. The first number gives the number of the Map and the second the dot on that map. The letters **OP** in the heading indicate a view point from which salient points of the battle are described. **RWC** indicates refreshment and toilet facilities. Travel directions are written in italics and indented to make them stand out clearly. An end point is suggested, with a total distance and timing without deviations or refreshment stops.

In addition **Extra Visits** are described to sites of particular interest which lie near to the route of the main itineraries. These are tinted light grey and boxed so that they clearly stand out from the main route. Estimates of the round-trip mileage and duration are given. Small deviations to other points of interest are described thus: **[N.B...]**

It is absolutely essential to **SET YOUR MILEAGE TRIP TO ZERO** before starting and to make constant reference to it. Odometers can vary from car to car and where you park or turn round will affect your total so that it may differ slightly from that given in this book. What is important, however, is the distance between stops. Distances in the headings are given in miles because the trip meters on British cars still operate in miles. Distances within the text are sometimes given in kilometres and metres as local signposts use these measures.

Stout waterproof footwear and clothing, binoculars and a torch are recommended. Make sure you take adequate supplies of any medication that you are on. Basic picnic gear can prove most useful. A mobile phone is a reassuring accessory.

Maps/Choosing Your Routes/Particular Visits

Below we recommend some commercial maps for the Battlefield Tour and it is suggested that the traveller buys them, or their nearest updated equivalent, and marks them before setting out. These maps, used in conjunction with the sketch maps in this book, make it possible not only to navigate efficiently but also to understand what happened where - and sometimes 'why'. We also suggest the use of the very detailed *Major & Mrs Holt's Battle Map of The Ypres Salient* and the sketch maps which accompany the three battles described in this book use the same colour coding system of mauve for war cemeteries, yellow for memorials, blue for museums, pink for bunkers and craters, orange for demarcation stones.

For an excellent overall view of all the battlefields in this book the Michelin 236 Nord Flandres-Artois Picardie 1/200,000 – 1 cm : 2kms is highly recommended.

An approximate distance from Calais is given to the start point.

Specific places to be visited may be found by reference to the Index and if a particular grave is to be located you should consult the Commonwealth War Graves Commission Debt of Honour website, the American Battlefield Monuments Commission website, the Australian War Memorial Roll of Honour or the Canadian Maple Leaf Legacy Project (pages 97-101) before you set out.

List of Maps

Legend for Maps

Bunkers	●	Place locations	▲
Demarcation Stones	●	Sites of Special Interest	○
Memorials	●	War Cemeteries	●
Museums	●		

At the end of the book the 'Tourist Information' section gives tips on how to prepare for your journey, where to eat or stay, and where you will find information and help. The 'War Graves Organisations' section gives contacts for the dedicated associations which tend and administer the war cemeteries and memorials that you visit by following the tours. Other Commemorative Associations are listed.

Place Names

Note that there is considerable and often confusing variation in place names created by the disparate Flemish and French versions of the same place name, e.g. Mesen and Messines, Ieper and Ypres, Kortrijk and Courtrai, Rijsel and Lille, Doornik and Tournai, Nieuwkerke and Neuve Eglise, Waasten and Warneton etc. Also the names of CWGC Cemeteries tend to employ the French version of place names used in the war. Thus we have 'Wytschaete' Mil Cemetery in Wijtschate, and 'Westoutre' Cemeteries in Westouter. During the war Elverdinge, Geluveld, Hooge, Poperinge, Vlamertinge had an 'h' after their 'g'. Nieuport was Nieuwpoort, Diksmuide was Dixmude, the Ijzer was the Yser – and so on.

Countdown to War

*'The lights are going out all over Europe,
we shall not see them lit again in our lifetime'.*
Edward, Viscount Grey of Fallodon

On 28 June 1914 Archduke Franz Ferdinand and his wife were assassinated at Sarajevo in Bosnia. The Archduke was the heir apparent to the throne of the Austro-Hungarian Empire, then ruled by the Emperor Franz Josef. He had gone to Austrian-occupied Bosnia on a tour designed to bolster up the Empire which was cracking under a rising tide of ethnic nationalism. The assassins were Serbs and the Austrians immediately accused the Kingdom of Serbia of harbouring the killers and others like them, and determined upon revenge. It also seemed an opportunity to crush the growing strength of the Serbs.

On 23 July the Austrians sent an ultimatum to Serbia demanding that anti-Austrian propaganda should be banned in Serbia and that the man behind the assassination be found and arrested. To these points the Serbs agreed, but they did not agree to having Austrian officials in their country to supervise the proceedings. On 28 July the Austrians, considering the response to be unsatisfactory, declared war on Serbia.

Now the dominoes began to fall as old loyalties, tribal relationships and treaties toppled country after country into one armed camp or the other. Germany sided with Austria, Russia with Serbia. The French, still hurting from their defeat by Prussia in 1870 and determined to regain from Germany their lost provinces of Alsace-Lorraine, saw a victorious war as a method of achieving that objective.

On 31 July Russia ordered general mobilisation followed that same day by Austria. The British Foreign Secretary, Sir Edward Grey, asked both France and Germany if they would observe Belgian neutrality. France replied 'Yes'. The Germans remained silent and the Belgians ordered that mobilisation should begin the following day.

On 1 August the French ordered mobilisation, Belgium announced her intention of remaining neutral and Germany declared war on Russia. On 2 August German troops invaded Luxembourg and made small sorties into France. Belgium refused to allow German forces to cross her soil with the object of 'anticipating' (as the Germans put it or, as in the case of Iraq in 2003, making a 'pre-emptive strike') a French attack and the King of the Belgians appealed to King George V of Britain for help.

On 3 August, Bank Holiday Monday, Germany declared war on France, while in Britain bright sunshine warmed the holiday crowds and Sir Edward Grey told Parliament, that 'we cannot issue a declaration of unconditional neutrality'.

On 4 August, just after 0800 hours, German forces crossed into Belgium. The British issued mobilisation orders and the British Ambassador in Berlin told the Chancellor that unless Germany withdrew her troops by midnight their countries would be at war with one another.

The Germans did not withdraw. It was war.

The Schlieffen Plan

The German plan for the conquest of France began to evolve in the early 1890s under the direction of the chief of Staff, Field Marshal Count von Schlieffen. France and Russia, between whom Germany was effectively sandwiched, were allied against possible German aggression under the Dual Alliance of 1892 and so Schlieffen had to devise a plan that avoided fighting both enemies at the same time. According to German military intelligence estimates the Russians would be unable to mobilise fully for six weeks after the beginning of a war. Therefore, reasoned Schlieffen, if France were to be attacked first and defeated within six weeks, Germany could then turn around and take on Russia. That logic, however, only moved the goal posts to uncover another challenge: how to defeat France in six weeks?

Schlieffen had the answer to that too. The key element to a quick victory was surprise and simplistically the plan aimed to fool the French into maintaining their major forces in the area of Alsace-Lorraine to counter an invasion directly from Germany around Metz, while the actual assault descended on France from the north via neutral Belgium.

Ten German divisions were nominated to keep an eye on the Russians, while 62 were assembled to take on the French. Of these latter, five armies were assembled in a line facing west and stretching northwards from Metz (see **Map 1**, page 19) to form a door hinged upon Switzerland. This door was to swing in a massive anti-clockwise movement through Belgium. At the top of the door was von Kluck's 1st Army and von Schlieffen had enjoined that the very last soldier at the end of the swing should 'brush the Channel with his sleeve'.

Von Schlieffen died in 1912, saying on his deathbed, 'Above all, keep the right wing strong'. His successor was Helmut von Moltke, nephew of the von Moltke of the 1870 War but made of different stuff to his eminent ancestor. A cautious man, lacking the ruthlessness upon which Schlieffen's plan depended and frightened by the possibility of a strong counter-attack by the French in the area of Alsace-Lorraine, he strengthened the hinge end of the door, thus weakening the force at the other end that was planned to sweep through Belgium.

Nevertheless, when the invasion began, von Moltke had almost 1.5 million men forming his door and at the far end of his extreme right wing, there was the 1st Army, commanded by General von Kluck, who saw himself as Attila the Hun.

General von Kluck, Commander Ger 1st Army, wounded 1915, retired October 1916, died 1934.

On 4 August 1914 the door began to swing and Attila invaded Belgium.

FIRST YPRES

18 OCTOBER-11 NOVEMBER 1914

'Shall I ever forget this day?
It will be indelibly stamped on my memory.
How anyone survived to tell the story is a mystery to me.'
An infantry Captain at Gheluvelt.

'You see why you should walk lightly if you ever go to Ypres,
the very stones of which are memorials to men
who perished on the Field of Honour.'
Maj J.M. Halley, 62nd Field Coy, RE.

SUMMARY OF THE BATTLE

In an attempt to break through the rapidly stabilising allied line and to reach Calais, von Falkenhayn launched the 4th and 6th (Ger) Armies against the BEF at Ypres on 18 October 1914. The fighting, toe to toe, staggered on with no real advantage gained by either side until heavy rains brought the contest to an end on 11 November. The British lost 2,350 officers and 55,800 soldiers. German losses were more than 130,000.

OPENING MOVES

Following II Corps' brief encounter at le Cateau the BEF continued its retreat from Mons and crossed the River Marne on 3 September. Von Kluck, believing that the Allies were beaten, altered the main thrust of his attack to come east of Paris and crossed the river only a day after the BEF. This change of direction exposed his right flank (doubtless von Schlieffen turned in his grave) and on 6 September the French 6th Army struck at it with 150,000 men, while the remainder of the Allies, including the BEF, about faced and drove the Germans 40 miles back to the Aisne River. The Schlieffen Plan was finished. Its failure was probably due to Von Moltke's steady weakening of the German right wing,

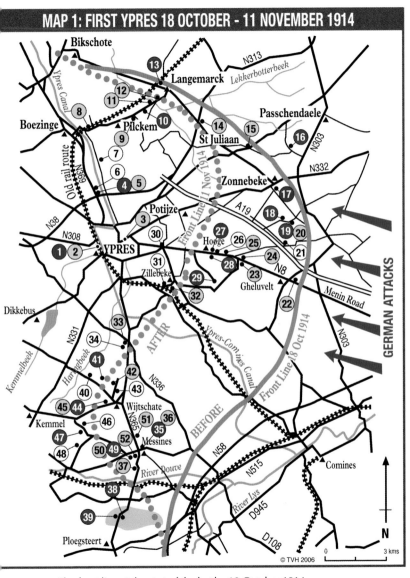

MAP 1: FIRST YPRES 18 OCTOBER - 11 NOVEMBER 1914

Bikschote

13

Langemarck

N313

Lekkerbotterbeek

12

11

8

10

Passchendaele

Boezinge

9

Pilckem

14

St Juliaan

15

16

N303

7

6

4

5

Zonnebeke

N332

17

Potijze

3

30

27

Hooge

26 25

18

19 20

A19

YPRES

31

28

24

21

Zillebeke

29

23

22

Gheluvelt

N8

32

Menin Road

Dikkebus

33

AFTER

34

Ypres-Comines Canal

GERMAN ATTACKS

41

42

N336

40

45 44

43

Kemmel

46

51 36

Wijtschate

47

50 49

52

35

Messines

N58

48

37

BEFORE

Front Line 18 Oct 1914

N515

Comines

N303

River Douve

38

River Lys

D945

39

Ploegsteert

D108

N

0   3 kms

© TVH 2006

—— The front line at the start of the battle, 18 October 1914
••••• The front line at the end of the battle, 11 November 1914

Legend for Map 1

1. The In Flanders Fields Museum
2. St George's Mem Church
3. The Menin Gate Mem
4. Essex Farm CWGC
5. John McCrae and 43 Div Memorials
6. John McCrae's Dressing Station
7. Yorkshire Trench
8. Breton Mem
9. Hedd Wyn Mem Plaque
10. Cement House CWGC
11. Steenbeek Albertina Mem
12. 20th Light Div Mem
13. German Cemetery Langemarck
13a. Pte Dancox VC Mem Namur
14. Canadian Brooding Soldier Mem
15. New Zealand Mem
16. Tyne Cot CWGC & Visitor Centre
17. Mem Museum Zonnebeke
17a. Scottish Mem, Frezenberg
18. Polygon Wood CWGC Cem
19. Buttes New British CWGC Cem
20. Australian 5th Div Mem & New Zealand Mem to the Missing
21. Black Watch Corner
22. South Wales Borderers & 2nd Bn Worcesters Mem
23. 18th Eastern Div Mem
24. Gloucester Regt Mem
25. Kings Royal Rifle Corps Mem
26. Hooge crater and trenches
27. Hooge Museum
28. Hooge CWGC Cem
29. Sanctuary Wood Museum and trenches
30. Hellfire Corner
31. Hill 60 Museum
32. 14th Light Div, Queen Victoria's Rifles & 1st Australia Tunnelling Coy Memorials
33. Tunnellers Mem St Eloi
34. Crater St Eloi
35. Museum Messines
36. New Zealand Kowhai tree, Ross Bastiaan plaque and Mié Tabe Peace Post
37. Island of Ireland Peace Tower
38. Hyde Park Corner CWGC Cem
39. Ploegsteert Mem & Berkshire CWGC Extension Cem
40. Hollandseschuur Craters
41. Croonaert Chapel CWGC Cem
42. 1st CAP Mem
43. Bayernwald Trenches etc
44. Wytschaete Mil CWGC Cem
45. 16th Irish Div Mem
46. Spanbroekmolen Crater
47. Lone Tree CWGC Cem
48. Kruisstraat Craters
49. Messines Ridge Brit CWGC Cem
50. NZ Mem
51. London Scottish Mem
52. NZ Mem Park
53. Prowse Point CWGC Cem
54. Christmas Truce Cross
55. Bairnsfather Plaque

Features on the route of the Battlefield Tour from start to finish

contrary to Schlieffen's death-bed plea to 'keep it strong'. On 14 September he was replaced by General Eric von Falkenhayn.

That same day, 14 September, General Joffre began an attack on the German positions beyond the Aisne with the BEF and the French 5th and 6th Armies. The gains against the well-entrenched Germans were small and after two days Joffre began moving forces to the north-west in an attempt to get around the end of the German line. Von Falkenhayn responded by moving reserves to outflank the outflankers who responded in similar measure. The line grew and grew in a 'race to the sea' which ended when the Allies reached the coast at Nieuwpoort in Belgium in the first week of October 1914.

The BEF moved north in the 'race' in two parts: II Corps went directly to la Bassée and immediately came into action on 11 October in the 25-mile gap south of Ypres and I Corps went first to St Omer where the C-in-C, Sir John French, had to make a choice. Either I Corps should go further to the north where thinly stretched French forces together with the recently arrived British 7th Division were maintaining their hold on Ypres and their contact with the Belgians on the coast, or he should reinforce II Corps at la Bassée. He sent I Corps to Ypres and the First Battle began.

WHAT HAPPENED

Le Cateau was the last of the old-style one-day battles. The fighting at Ypres was never so simple. The title 'First Ypres' seems to describe a clear-cut contest, over a set period, with an agreed victor, yet by the end of 1914 the measure of victory was changing. It was no longer 'he who held the ground' but 'he who had the will to fight' who prevailed, and the will depended upon many things, including national reserves of manpower. 'Kill the enemy' became not just a tactical requirement but a strategic necessity. Everywhere, all the time, each side was intent upon killing the other. 'All Quiet Along the Potomac Tonight', goes the haunting song from the American Civil War, which goes on to intone that the loss of 'a private or two now and again will not count in the news of the battle'. That daily loss, even when there was no official 'battle' in progress, became significant during the First World War.

It was never 'All Quiet on the Western Front'. The BEF would lose hundreds of men by 'natural wastage' every day from 1915 onwards, yet every so often the enemies lumbered dinosaur-like into battle against each other and engaged in periods of ferocious killing that were graced with distinctive names. So it was with 'First Ypres', where the blood of a quarter of a million soldiers began etching a line of trenches that would stretch from the North Sea to Switzerland. Yet when the battle began (and historians cannot agree on the exact date) the leaders were still hoping for a great victory, a decisive battle. It was not to be.

The armchair analyst can divide First Ypres into neat and separate parts:

Battle of Armentières	13 Oct-2 Nov
Battle of Messines	12 Oct-2 Nov
Battle of Langemarck	21 Oct-24 Oct
Battle of Gheluvelt	29 Oct-31 Oct
Battle of Nonne Boschen	11 Nov

These classifications are geographical and the actions associated with them are best described during the battlefield tour below which, to simplify touring, covers First, Second and Third Ypres simultaneously. Running together the October and November actions, the 'First' Battle of Ypres is generally accepted to have opened on 18 October 1914 when the Germans began a three-week period of repeated mass attacks against the British positions. The British occupied a salient which bulged forward with a 16 mile-long perimeter into the German line (see **Map 1**). The heart of the Salient was Ypres, its defence now the responsibility of I Corps, and German attacks were concentrated along the axis of the Menin Road which enters Ypres from the east, passing as it does so the hamlet of Gheluvelt, barely 8 miles from Ypres Cathedral.

On 31 October Gheluvelt was lost and the Germans were on the brink of breaking through the line, outflanking the BEF and making a run for the Channel Ports. In one of the most remarkable actions of the War the 2nd Worcesters charged the enemy at Gheluvelt and saved the day. The Germans made one more major effort along the same axis when on 11 November 12$\frac{1}{2}$ divisions attacked across a 9-mile front with almost 18,000 men against 8,000. It wasn't enough. On that day, weighted down with mud and casualties, the First Battle of Ypres ended. The Salient perimeter had shrunk to 11 miles, but Ypres had not fallen. It never would.

Memorial to 2nd Worcesters, Gheluvelt.

THE BATTLEFIELD TOUR

This is done in conjunction with Second and Third Ypres. See **Maps 1, 2 and 3**, page 19, page 26 and page 30.

SECOND YPRES

22 APRIL–25 MAY 1915

'There was a curious smell, which was quite noticeable – we all remarked on it – and then after a time the casualties started coming in. It was most dramatic: long, long lines of Canadian soldiers, single file, each man with his hand on the shoulder of the man in front. There would be a man in front who could see – all these other chaps couldn't; hundreds and hundreds of these chaps stumbling along, single file.'
A First World War Doctor.

'Of one's feelings all this night – of the asphyxiated French soldiers – of the women and children – of the cheery steady British reinforcements that moved up quietly past us going up, not back – I could write, but you can imagine.'
Col John McCrea.

SUMMARY OF THE BATTLE

At around 1700 hours on 22 April 1915 the Germans attacked the north-eastern edge of the Ypres Salient using poison gas in what is generally accepted as the first major use of gas in warfare. Subsequent defensive fighting against repeated gas attacks resulted in a shortened Salient, but no breakthrough. Allied casualties were about 60,000, German 35,000.

OPENING MOVES

At the end of 1914, the German General Staff decided that, having failed to defeat France quickly and now being faced by enemies in both the east and the west, they would concentrate upon the Russian front. General Erich von Falkenhayn considered that Russia, struggling with internal political discontent, was the weaker of his two immediate protagonists and would succumb to concentrated German might. As far as the Western Front was concerned he instructed his commanders only to do enough 'lively activity' to keep the enemy occupied. One of the things that seemed likely to 'occupy' the French and British was to try out poison gas on them.

Article 23 of the 1907 Hague Convention, which Germany had signed, forbade the use of 'poisons or poisonous weapons', but before April 1915 the Germans had already tried out gas. Shrapnel shells containing a form of chemical irritant were tried out near Neuve Chapelle in October 1914 and tear gas shells had been used at Bolimow in Poland in January 1915, but neither trial produced any significant result. Von Falkenhayn was, however, supportive of the idea of developing a gas weapon and extensive testing was carried out at the Kummersdorf artillery ranges near Berlin. In the Second World War another secret weapon was tested there – von Braun's V2 rocket.

Germany possessed the most powerful chemical industry in the world and it was not difficult to consider other ways than shelling in which an enemy might be enveloped in a gas cloud. What was more difficult was to decide where to use the gas and several German commanders considered the use of such a weapon to be unethical. However, Falkenhayn persisted and, keeping in mind his need to draw attention away from his intended effort in the east, he looked for a sensitive spot on the Western Front. Ypres was such a place.

The 4th (Ger) Army had been on the edge of breaking through during First Ypres (cf. Gheluvelt p.62) and the Salient was the only significant piece of Belgian soil not yet occupied. Added benefits were that the BEF had been decimated in defending Ypres and any activity there would demand wholehearted British attention as well as the fact that the French knew full well that holding Ypres was the key to keeping the Germans out of the Pas de Calais. Therefore Duke Albrecht of Würtemberg and his 4th (Ger) Army facing Ypres were chosen to try out the new weapon. Preparations began in February 1915.

The simplest method of delivery of the gas was by cylinder, since that was the standard commercial container. Train loads of the heavy 3.5ft long objects were brought into the lines. It is estimated that some 30,000 cylinders were brought up into the forward areas and inevitably some were damaged – by accident or enemy action – so that the presence of the gas weapon was fairly common knowledge among German soldiers as time went on. Now and again German prisoners were taken who spoke about the presence of gas. However neither the French nor the British authorities took the reports seriously enough to take any precautions, though early in April Canadian troops were warned about the possibility of a gas attack following the mention of gas in the French 10th Army's 30 March intelligence bulletin.

The cylinders were dug into their firing positions in groups of 20, each group covering 40 yards of front and, 24 hours ahead of the intended assault time, the German soldiers were given their final briefings. At 0500 hours on 22 April 1915 everything was ready – except the wind. It was blowing the wrong way.

WHAT HAPPENED

As the German infantry waited, hoping for the wind to change direction, their field artillery pounded the front line defences and heavy 17-inch guns bombarded the rear areas. When the day matured it became warm and sunny, perhaps lulling the defenders into a degree of laxity and certainly making the Germans hot and uncomfortable in their heavy equipment. By late afternoon the attack was in the balance. Soon it would be dark. The offensive could not be made at night. Then, soon after 1600 hours a breeze began to develop from the north-east and one hour later the Germans opened the nozzles of thousands of gas cylinders and a fog of death rolled slowly across No Man's Land.

Below the Pilckem Ridge was the Canadian 3rd Brigade and alongside them, north of the ridge, the French Algerian 45th Colonial Division and it was upon these two formations that the fog descended. Sir Arthur Conan Doyle described what happened: 'The French troops, staring over the top of their parapet at this curious screen which ensured them a temporary relief from fire, were observed suddenly to throw up their hands, to clutch at their throats, and to fall to the ground in agonies of asphixiation. Many lay where they had fallen, while their comrades, absolutely helpless against this diabolical agency, rushed madly out of the mephitic mist and made for the rear, over-running the lines of the trenches behind them. Many of them never halted until they had reached Ypres, while others rushed westwards and put the canal between themselves and the enemy.'

By 1900 hours there was no organised body of French troops east of the Ypres Canal (see Map 2). Between the Belgians (who held the ground north of the 45th Division's area) and the Canadian 3rd Brigade there was now a gap of 8,000 yards. The way to Ypres was open. The German advance (four reserve divisions – the 45th, 46th, 51st and 52nd) was cautious and limited. Their objective had been to take the Pilckem Ridge and no more and by the time they reached it darkness was falling. Thus it was not until the following morning that they realised how successful their attack had been and just how close they were to Ypres, which they could now see quite clearly ahead of them. The Canadians around St Julien, meanwhile, had reacted to the gas with determination, despite the fact that the French panic had left their northern flank unprotected. Brigadier General R.E.W. Turner commanding the Canadian 3rd Brigade ordered his reserve battalion, the 14th, into line beside the already positioned 13th and 15th battalions and held strong German attacks north of Keerselare (cf 'The Brooding Soldier' Map 1/14) until they finally stopped at about 1830 hours. Two platoons of the 13th fought to their last man and **L/Cpl Frederick Fisher** of the battalion won a posthumous **VC** for his actions that day. His citation as published in the

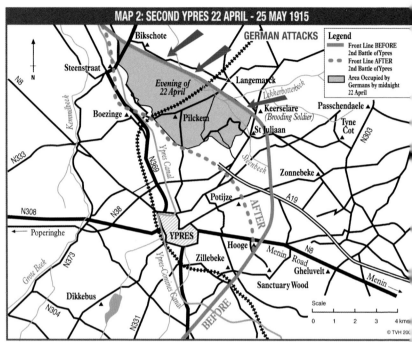

MAP 2: SECOND YPRES 22 APRIL - 25 MAY 1915

GERMAN ATTACKS

Legend
Front Line BEFORE 2nd Battle of Ypres
Front Line AFTER 2nd Battle of Ypres
Area Occupied by Germans by midnight 22 April

Bikschote
Steenstraat
Evening of 22 April
Langemarck
Lekkerbotterbeek
Passchendaele
Boezinge
Pilckem
Keerselare (Brooding Soldier)
St Juliaan
Tyne Cot
Zonnebeke
Steenbeek
Potijze
A19
AFTER
N369
Ypres Canal
Kemmelbeek
N8
N333
N308
N38
Poperinghe
YPRES
Hooge
Menin Road
Gheluvelt
Menin
N8
Zillebeke
Sanctuary Wood
Grote Beek
N373
Ypres-Comines Canal
BEFORE
Dikkebus
N304
N331
Scale
0 1 2 3 4 kms
© TVH 200

London Gazette gives the date of his action as the 23rd, but Canadian authorities say that this is incorrect. Sir Max Aitken, the Canadian Record Officer, later (as Lord Beaverbrook) wrote *Canada in Flanders*, the story of Canadian actions to 1916, including an entire chapter, with maps, covering the gas attacks.

Curiously, the fact that the Canadians stood and fought through the gas attack meant that they suffered less from it than they might have done had they followed the example of the French colonial troops and streamed back to the rear. The Official History explains: 'It early became evident that the men who stayed in their places suffered less than those who ran away, any movement making worse the effects of the gas, and those who stood up on the fire step suffered less – indeed they often escaped any serious effects – than those who lay down or sat at the bottom of a trench. Men who stood on the parapet suffered least, as the gas was denser near the ground. The worst sufferers were the wounded lying on the ground, or on stretchers, and the men who moved back with the cloud.'

General Smith-Dorrien commanding the 2nd Army first heard news of the attack at about 1845 hours on the 22nd and immediate moves were made to bring up reinforcements to plug the line. General Foch heard at midnight what had happened and reacted typically with three steps that should be taken: (1) hold; (2) organise for a counter-attack; (3) counter-attack. In fact counter-attacks did begin that night and following Foch's proposals it was agreed that 'vigorous action' east of the canal would be the best way to check any German attempts to advance. The enemy, however, struck first and on 24 April following a one-hour heavy bombardment the Germans

How a gas attack may have looked.

released a gas cloud at 0400 hours immediately to the north-east of Keerselare and on a front of 1,000 yards against the Canadian Division. Throughout the day pressure on the Canadians forced them to withdraw to second-line positions, Keerselare being captured early in the afternoon. The following day, Sunday, 25 April 1915, the day of the Gallipoli landings, the Germans made a fierce effort to break the British lines. They made gains, but they did not break through.

The struggle continued in a series of engagements classified as the Battle of s-Gravenstafel, 22-23 April; Battle of St Julien, 24 April-5 May; Battle of Frezenberg, 8-13 May and Battle of Bellewaerde, 24-25 May. Overall the Germans made net gains. On 4 May the British made tactical withdrawals in order to shorten their lines, reducing their frontage from 21,000 yards to 16,000 yards and shortening the greatest depth of the Salient from 9,000 to 5,000 yards. In the World of 'If', the Germans might have taken Ypres and then the Channel Ports: if they had not used the gas just as a tactical distraction, but part of a major attack; if they had had reserves ready to follow up the initial success; if the wind had been in the right direction early on 22 April they would have seen how successful the gas had been and could have called up forces to exploit the break in the French lines. If they had used their secret weapon properly, say many, they could have won the war with it. The 'after-the-event' experts say the same thing about the British use of the tank on the Somme. Perhaps the most relevant 'If' belongs to the Canadians, courtesy of Rudyard Kipling, because they kept their heads when all about were losing theirs.

THE BATTLEFIELD TOUR

This is done in conjunction with First and Third Ypres – see page 34.

THIRD YPRES
Passchendaele

7 JUNE-10 NOVEMBER 1917

*'Rain has turned everything into a quagmire and the shell holes
are full of water. Duckboards are everywhere leading to the front line,
but Jerry has these well taped and frequently shells them or sprays
them with indirect machine-gun fire. ... Guns of all calibres are
everywhere, in places wheel to wheel. The debris of war is lying about.
Broken guns, limbers, horses blown to blazes.
But very few human bodies, for they have all been swallowed up in
the mud and water of this horrible sector.
It seems madness on the part of Higher Authority to expect any
advance over this indescribable morass.'*
The diary of a Sergeant in the Somerset Light Infantry.

SUMMARY OF THE BATTLE

On 7 June 1917 the British attacked and captured the Messines Ridge, a
dominant feature that extended northwards to the German-held Passchendaele
Ridge. On 31 July, the British attacked again and floundered in mud and rain in
an assault that earned General Haig the title of 'Butcher' and won the
Passchendaele Ridge after 16 weeks' fighting. British losses were over 300,000
and German losses, never published, variously estimated between 65,000 and
260,000.

OPENING MOVES

Early in May 1917, following the bloody failure of Nivelle's attack on the Chemin
des Dames, the French Army began to mutiny until sixteen Army Corps were
involved. On 15 May, General Pétain, 'the saviour of Verdun', took Nivelle's
place and, by a mixture of personal visits to front line units and summary courts
martial, including executions, set about restoring discipline. Richard M. Watt, in
his book *Dare Call it Treason*, supposes that at least 100,000 men actively

mutinied and even the official figures admit that between May and October 1917 23,385 men were found guilty of offences. Yet, extraordinarily, the news of the mutinies did not become general knowledge.

Haig therefore realised that the French would have to be left out of any immediate British plans for an offensive and later asserted that Pétain actually asked him to maintain British attacks on the Germans in order to relieve pressure on the French. Haig had fought his first battle as C-in-C the previous year on the Somme and opinions were sharply divided about its outcome – whether it had been a strategic success in the casualties inflicted upon the Germans, or a costly failure because of our own losses. Nevertheless, Haig was still determined to prove himself as a commander. His conviction that the only way to win the war was by frontal assault remained undimmed. If he wanted to win the war alone he had to hurry, because on 6 April 1917 America had declared war on Germany and soon her soldiers would arrive to swing the balance against the Germans.

Thus to 'help' the French, to prove himself and his men, and to do it before the Americans arrived, he set about planning an attack. First though, he had to persuade a reluctant War Committee that an attack was both needed and would have positive results. The War Cabinet, which had to sanction the C-in-C's plans, was led by the Prime Minister, Lloyd George, who was very unhappy at the long British casualty lists for which he held Haig personally responsible. Haig promised that his campaign would be a limited one and proposed that it should be in Flanders in order to capture the German U-Boat bases on the Belgian coast, said by the Admiralty to be the source of the submarine offensive. In fact the U-Boats were coming from Germany and the Belgian theory surprised many people, including the chief of Haig's intelligence staff who later said, 'No one really believed this rather amazing view.'

However, Haig found it useful and when he maintained that 'if the fighting was kept up at its present intensity for six months, Germany would be at the end of her available manpower', the War Committee reluctantly agreed to his plans.

First of all the C-in-C wanted to gain a foothold at the southern end of the Ypres Salient, around a village called Messines. It was to be a remarkably successful battle that by its very success may have doomed General Gough's 5th Army to the seemingly endless slog up the slope to Passchendaele.

WHAT HAPPENED

The high ground at the southern end of the Salient had been occupied by the Germans since the British shortened their lines at the end of Second Ypres. The

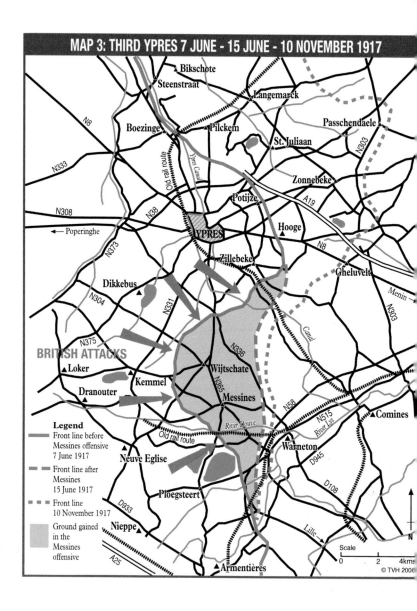

MAP 3: THIRD YPRES 7 JUNE - 15 JUNE - 10 NOVEMBER 1917

Bikschote

Steenstraat

Langemarck

Boezinge

Pilckem

Passchendaele

St. Juliaan

N8

N333

Old rail route

Ypres Canal

N38

Zonnebeke

N303

N308

Potijze

A19

◄--- Poperinghe

N373

YPRES

Hooge

N8

Zillebeke

Gheluvelt

Dikkebus

Menin

N304

N331

N303

N375

Canal

BRITISH ATTACKS

N336

▲ Loker

Wijtschate

Kemmel

N365

Dranouter

Messines

N58

Comines

River Douve

N515

River Lys

Legend

Old rail route

Warneton

D945

Front line before
Messines offensive
7 June 1917

Neuve Eglise

Front line after
Messines
15 June 1917

D108

Ploegsteert

Front line
10 November 1917

D933

Lille ►

Ground gained
in the
Messines
offensive

Nieppe

Scale

N

0   2   4kms

A25

Armentières

© TVH 2006

Messines-Wijtschate area was of particular value to the Germans because from there they could enfilade much of the British trench system. The task of dislodging them was given to General Plumer's 2nd Army. Plumer had already been preparing for an assault for over a year by tunnelling under the German lines and placing 19 huge mines in a ten-mile arc from near Hill 60 via Spanbroekmolen to Ploegsteert Wood. There were over four miles of tunnels and more than a million pounds of high explosives. The attack was planned in great detail and models of the German positions used so that formations down to company level could be quite clear what their objectives were, and those objectives were limited and precise.

At 0310 on 7 June 1917 the mines exploded following more than two weeks bombardment by over 2,000 guns. X (British) Corps and II (Anzac) Corps advanced, assisted by 72 tanks and with complete air superiority. By the end of the day the first objectives were all taken. The 36th (Ulster) Division and the 16th (Irish) Division took Wijtschate and Messines fell to the New Zealanders.

So far so good. So now on to the Passchendaele Ridge while the momentum of success was still warm? No. Now a near 8 weeks delay while preparations were made for the next attack. Why wasn't the Messines attack delayed until it could be followed immediately by the second phase? Were the French in such desperate straits that we had to grasp the German's attention in June? Perhaps. Perhaps too we needed to assemble and to reposition our artillery, something not done in a few hours, but the delay was fateful. It saw out the good weather and gave the Germans time to put the finishing touches to their new scheme of defence – defence in depth. Gone now were the old linear lines. Now trenches ran backwards and forwards in great depth and within the grid so formed were disconnected strongpoints and concrete pillboxes. The manning philosophy had changed too. The ground was covered by mutually supporting machine guns and forward positions were lightly held with reserves well back and concentrated ready for counter-attack. On top of all that the Germans introduced mustard gas.

The preliminary bombardment began on 22 July 1917. Over 3,000 guns hurled almost five tons of shells at every yard of the front. Ten days later, at 0350 hours on 31 July, twelve divisions advanced on an 11-mile front in pouring rain.

North of Ypres advances of two miles were made, the Pilckem Ridge was recaptured, but further south and around the Menin Road the attack quickly stuck. The preliminary bombardment had totally destroyed the water table and the rain could not run away. Shell holes filled to overflowing with water and the earth turned into a thick glutinous mud, stinking and foul with the decay of dead horses and thousands of corpses. The mud reached out and sucked under any unwary soldier who left the duckboard path. Gough advised Haig that the attack should be stopped, but the C-in-C, falsely buoyant from the success at Messines, perhaps, or determined to demonstrate what Clausewitz called the 'maintenance of the Aim', i.e. steadfastness of purpose, pressed on, through battle after battle and casualty after casualty.

The Official History records the following battles:

Messines 7-14 June

Pilckem 31 July-2 Aug

Langemarck 16-18 Aug

Menin Road 20-25 Sept

Polygon Wood 26 Sept-3 Oct

Broodseinde 4 Oct

Poelcapelle 9 Oct

1st Passchendaele 12 Oct

2nd Passchendaele 26 Oct-10 Nov

In the first week of November, 16 weeks after the second phase began, the 1st and 2nd Canadian Divisions occupied the shapeless ruins of Passchendaele village. The mud and blood bath was over. It is said that Lt-Gen. Sir Launcelot Kiggell, Haig's Chief of Staff, visited the battlefield for the first time just after the fighting was over (a terrible indictment in itself) and when he saw the foul swamp in which it had been fought burst into tears saying, 'Good God! Did we really send men to fight in this?'

Current scenes from the interior of the In Flanders Fields Museum.

THE SALIENT BATTLEFIELD TOUR:
1st, 2nd, 3rd YPRES

Although the Three Battles of Ypres are normally identified and treated separately as historical bites, it is not possible to tour them in isolation. Therefore the battlefield tour described here is a tour of the Ypres Salient and encompasses all three battles (see **Map 1**, page 19). To tour the Salient in a comprehensive manner requires at least three days and travellers with that amount of time are referred to our guide book *Major & Mrs Holt's Battlefield Guide to the Ypres Salient and Passchendaele* with its accompanying detailed *Battle Map*. The following suggested tour covers the most important and easily accessible points of interest in the Salient.

The Route: The tour of First, Second and Third Ypres begins at the In Flanders Fields Museum in Ypres, visits St George's Memorial Church and the Menin Gate Memorial by foot. It then moves north and clockwise via Essex Farm; Yorkshire Trench, Boezinge; Langemarck German Cemetery & Interpretative Centre; the Canadian Brooding Soldier Memorial; Plaque to 15th Bn, 48th Highlanders of Canada; Tyne Cot British Cemetery & Interpretative Centre, KOYLI and Notts & Derbys Memorials; Passchendaele Memorial Museum, Zonnebeke; Polygon Wood & Buttes New Brit Cemeteries, Australian 5th Div Memorial and N Zealand Memorial to the Missing; Black Watch Corner & Memorial to New Zealander Sgt H.J.Nicholas, VC, MM; Gheluvelt Mill & Memorials; Clapham Junction Memorials; KRRC Memorial; Hooge Crater, Preserved Trenches, Museum & Cemetery; Sanctuary Wood CWGC Cemetery and Museum & preserved trenches; Hellfire Corner; Hill 60 & Memorials; St Eloi Tunnellers' Memorial & Craters; Wijtschate – Bayern Wood, Croonaert Chapel CWGC Cemetery, 1st Chasseurs à Pied Memorial, Site of Hitler Painting; Wytschaete Military CWGC Cemetery/16th Irish & 36th (Ulster) Divs Memorials; Spanbroekmolen (Pool of Peace); Lone Tree CWGC Cemetery; Kruisstraat Craters; Messines Ridge British CWGC Cemetery/New Zealand Memorial; Messines Museum & Memorials; Island of Ireland Tower; Ploegsteert Memorial & Berks & Hyde Park Corner Cemeteries; Menin Gate.

Extra Visits: Lijssenthoek CWGC Mil Cemetery; Talbot House, Poperinge; Chavasse VC Memorial and Grave, Brandhoek; The London Scottish Memorial, Messines; Plugstreet Wood and St Yvon – Prowse Point CWGC Cemetery, Khaki Chums Christmas Truce Cross, Bairnsfather Memorial Plaque.

'N.B.s': Harry Patch Mem, Steenbeek; 34th Div Mem & Bunker, Dancox VC Memorial, Langemarck; Guynemer & Tank Mems, Poelkapelle; Plaque to Lt

Edward Donald Bellew VC, Vancouver Corner; Menin Road Museum. Churchill Plaque, Ploegsteert.

Total distance (excluding Extra Visits and 'N.B.' deviations): 55 miles
Total time: (excluding Extra Visits, 'N.B.' deviations, refreshment stops and time for Ypres walking tour) 9 hours
* **Distance from Calais to start point:** 59 miles. No Motorway Tolls
* **Base towns:** Ieper, Poperinge
* **Maps:** *Major & Mrs Holt's Battle Map of the Ypres Salient* plus best of all are the Carte de Belgique 1:25,000 Nos. 20/5-6, 28/1-2, 28/3-4, and 28/5-6. The Carte de Belgique No. 28 IEPER 1:50,000 is coloured and covers the whole area and shows the road changes, including the motorway up to 1979. IGN 2 Lille/Dunkerque 1:100,000 covers the area.

> *From Calais take the A16/A26 signed Dunkerque. At Grande Synthe take Exit 28 to the A25 to the right signed Lille, Ypres. Take Exit 13 at Steenvoorde on the D948 signed Ypres (Ieper). Cross the border (no longer manned) and continue on the D948/N38.*

Extra Visit to Lijssenthoek Military CWGC Cemetery, Talbot House, Poperinge and Chavasse VC Memorial and Grave, Brandhoek
Length of trip: 21.4miles. Approximate time: 45 minutes
> *Turn right signed to Lijssenthoek CWGC Cemetery.*

Lijssenthoek Military CWGC Cemetery. Lat & Long: 50.82840 2.701661.
The second largest CWGC Cemetery in Belgium (after Tyne Cot), beautifully designed by Sir Reginald Blomfield, it contains 9,901 Commonwealth WW1 burials plus 1 CWGC employee, only 24 being unidentified, and 883 other nationalities - French, German, Chinese and American. Among them is **Staff Nurse N. Spindler** of the QA; the well-loved **Rev Charles Edmund Doudney**; **Maj-Gen M. Smith Mercer**, 3 Can Div; **Brig-Gen H.G. Fitton** CB, DSO, 101st Inf Bde, 34th Div; **Brig-Gen A.F. Gordon** CMG, DSO, 153rd Inf Bde, 51st Highland Div; **Brig-Gen R.C. Gore**, CB, CMG, 101st Inf Bde, 34th Div. The cemetery (first used by the French in 1914) served the 4 Field Hospitals, covering 125 acres and number of CCSs, comprising some 4,000 hospital beds – hence the unusually small number of unidentified burials. The medical facilities grew up around Remy (or Remi) Farm and the sidings of the spur from the Poperinghe-Hazebrouck railway line.

In spring 2011 construction work starts on an unmanned **Visitor's Centre**, sited across the road from the small side entrance to the cemetery, with parking area and WC. It will tell the history of the Field Hospitals, of the CWGC (which has its nurseries adjacent to the cemetery) and of how the Cemetery is a mirror of what was happening at the front, as for every day of the year there is at least one grave. Personal stories and photos etc are being collected on a database system to tell a different 'Daily Story' 365 days of the year of men who are buried in this multinational cemetery. Visitors will be able to print out a plan of the cemetery showing the location of the subject of the day's story. Contact Annemie Morisse at lijssenthoek@poperinge.be if you can contribute any information and see also www.lijssenthoek.be

Lijssenthoek CWGC Cemetery

Return to the N38 and continue to the T junction with the R33 before Poperinge. Follow signs to Centrum and park near the main Market Square (undergoing archaeological excavations).

Known as 'the last stop before Hell', Poperinghe was the BEF's principal town behind the lines and was never taken by the Germans although it suffered occasional heavy shelling. The town teemed with shops, estaminets (segregated for officers and ORs), restaurants, hostels, concert halls, cabarets and cinemas, brothels and other facilities for the troops coming out of the line for rest and refreshment. The YMCA and the Church Army were well-represented. Today it makes a good base for touring the Salient.

In the square is the picturesque **Town Hall with the Tourist Office** in the basement. **Lat & Long: 50.85548 2.72713**. They have literature on Poperinghe (as it was spelt in 1914-18) during the Great War. Behind it are the Condemned Cells and the Execution Post where at least 5 men were shot during the war.

Walk to the far end of the square.

On the left at No 16 is the famous **Café de Ranke**, popular with officers during the war, mainly because of the charms of the daughter of the house, 'Ginger', and the liberally flowing champagne.

Walk up Gasthuisstraat.

Extra Visit continued

At No 12 was another popular officers' club, nicknamed Skindles.

Continue to No 43.

Talbot House. Lat & Long: 50.85593 2.72288

Still hanging outside the elegant building where Padre Philip Byard (Tubby) Clayton started a rest house which inspired the movement which is now world-wide, is a sign which states, 'Talbot House 1915-? Every Man's Club'. This extraordinary club was named after Gilbert Talbot, son of the Bishop of Winchester, who was killed in the Salient and is buried in Sanctuary Wood Cemetery (qv). Tommy shortened the name in Army signallers' language to 'Toc H'. It had the atmosphere of a home, where the men, weary and frightened from a spell in the trenches of the Salient, could come, whatever their rank, and be refreshed physically and spiritually.

Talbot House was officially opened on 11 December 1915, in the empty house of the banker and hop merchant, Maurice Coevoet Camerlynck. It operated on 'the Robin Hood principle of taking from the rich to give to the poor', maintained Tubby, another of whose occasional nicknames was 'Boniface' (after the innkeeper in George Farquhar's *The Beaux Stratagem*). Tubby had a marvellous knack of wheedling supplies, furniture and other domestic items from all and sundry, notably a famous piano. According to *Tales from Talbot House*, for 5 francs officers arriving from the leave train at one a.m. secured cocoa and Oliver biscuits or before departure at 5 a.m. a cold meat breakfast. Other ranks did not pay until June 1916 when the officers were 'thrown out' to Skindles (see above). Until then they (but never other ranks) could get a bed.

Only one soldier was killed in Talbot House during the war. He was Sgt G.J.M. Pegg, ASC CEF, who was mortally wounded by a shell that hit the side of The House on 28 May 1916. He is buried in Poperinghe New Mil Cemetery.

From April 1918 the Germans pressed ever closer to Ypres, Kemmel fell, defensive lines were hastily built around Poperinghe, great expanses of countryside between Dunkirk and St Omer were flooded. Poperinghe was evacuated of civilians; cinemas, shops and other entertainments closed down. Alone Toc H remained open. But it was heavily shelled and eventually 'imperative orders to leave at once' were received. It closed on Whit Tuesday, 21 May to re-open on 30 September at the end of Fourth Ypres.

Extra Visit continued

In 1919 Tubby founded the Toc H movement and in 1929 Lord Wakefield of Hythe, at the instigation of Major Paul Slessor (who gave his name, to the 'Slessorium' – originally a bath house for post-war pilgrims – built in the garden in 1930 and to whom there is a memorial plaque in the hall), put up sufficient funds to buy the Old House. He also bought the 'Pool of Peace' or Spanbroekmolen crater at Wijtschate (qv) for Toc H.

During World War II the Germans occupied Poperinghe on 29 May 1940. One report, as yet unconfirmed, says they requisitioned Talbot House on 13 July and in 1943 used it as billets for the Kriegsmarine. On 6 September 1944, Polish troops liberated the town and all the precious contents, whisked away by local sympathisers as the Germans moved in, were soon restored. On 10 September the house re-opened, with its original purpose to act as a rest house for British soldiers.

Many original artefacts, pictures (including portraits by one of the ninety-odd official war artists, Eric Kennington) and signs remain to be seen, witness of Tubby's relaxed attitude and the sense of humour which made him so special. 'All rank abandon ye who enter here' was his motto, inscribed over his, the Chaplain's, room...'

The chapel on the top floor, with its carpenter's bench which served as an altar, looks much the same as in the days when over 20,000 officers and soldiers received the Sacrament there before going into the trenches. In 1922 Barclay Baron, a founder member of Talbot House, suggested that the form of an early Christian lamp should become the symbol of Toc H ('as dim as a Toc H lamp' was a popular post-war phrase). The lamp was first lit by the Prince of Wales in 1923. In the well-tended, tranquil garden, which gave rest to many a man from the shattered landscape of the Salient, is an obelisk-shaped **Mié Tabé Peace Post** (qv) inaugurated on 24 September 1988.

On 24 October 1996, the Talbot House Association finally succeeded in purchasing the adjacent old hop store which Tubby had also used. Once more it forms an integral part of the Old House. The Association also owns and runs The House and provides guides and members of staff to look after it. Their Chief Executive is Mrs Annelies Vermeulen, e-mail talbot.house@skynet.be.

The House has had a succession of wardens and guides. For many years the most knowledgeable and enthusiastic guide was the popular Jacques Ryckebosch (now left) who did extensive research and spent much

Talbot House, Poperinge.

Memorial to Noel Chavasse, Double VC, Brandhoek Church.

Piano exhibit, Talbot House Museum.

Extra Visit continued

time cataloguing the treasures that still remain in the House. Much research has also been done by The Secretary, Mr Jan Louagie and his wife, authors of *Talbot House – Poperinghe, 'First Stop After Hell*. Research is ever continuing, e.g. on the 1,300 names written in the Toc H visitors' book of Dec '15-April '16 and in linking them with burials in Lijssenthoek Cemetery, by Dries Chaerle and his team who have produced the charming book *A Bed with Real Sheets* in period format, and by Annemie Morisse on the Lijssenthoek Project.

Talbot House provides clean and comfortable self-catering accommodation at a reasonable price. It makes an excellent base for touring the Salient. It is extremely popular – there is something very special about staying in this Club, so redolent of the Great War and the men who peopled it – and booking well in advance is advised.

Until 2003 The House was entered through the imposing front door in Gasthuisstraat but on 15 May 2004 the new reception area with a shop and toilets and the large exhibition area was opened in the old Hop Store with an entrance in Pottestraat (turn first right after the building on Gasthuisstraat). The old building has been extensively renovated and reinforced for the purpose. The exhibition is based on 'Life in the Poperinge area during The First World War' and is conceived as Tubby's 'photo album' showing the various aspects of life in the British sector. A new glass extension with a lift gives access to the first and second floors of the Hop Store and to the garden (in which there are some informative plaques). The Slessorium houses an audio-visual presentation in which Tubby shows the visitor around Talbot House plus some illustrations and documents on Little Talbot House in Ypres and Skindles. It includes Tubby's original 'hut' which was located at Proven in 'Dingley Dell'. On the first floor of the Hop Store the wartime Concert Hall has been restored to its 1917 aspect and shows a recreation of a wartime concert party (filmed with a live audience in January 2004). The second floor is used as a documentation and archives area and is not generally part of the regular visitor circuit but can be booked by school parties for lectures and working sessions.

These works have created much controversy with regular and faithful visitors to Talbot House who appreciated the delight of entering through the beautiful old front door to become immediately bathed in the warm

Extra Visit continued

glow of welcome created by Tubby in 1915 and which lingers still. Conscious of this, The Association gave them careful consideration but concluded that the changes had to be made for the very preservation of The House (a listed 18th Century building with a frail structure) itself. The changes are also designed to improve the quality of staying in The House. It was also considered that 'many visitors are unlikely to be aware of the traditions of the house and would not have any difficulty using an alternative entrance'.

On 12 November 2003 a special service was held for 105-year-old Arthur Halestrop, the only WW1 veteran who was able to travel to the Salient for the Armistice Day commemorations that year. It was a very moving occasion and local firemen took a day's unpaid leave to carry Arthur tenderly up the almost perpendicular staircase to the chapel on the top floor, so redolent with memories of the men who had said their last prayers in the room. In March 2008 the Poet Laureate Andrew Motion wrote a poem entitled, *The Five Acts of Harry Patch*, to honour Harry Patch the only surviving veteran of the Passchendaele battle and whose 110th birthday was on 17 June. Harry died on 25 July 2009, age 111 years, 1 month, 1 week, 1 day, then verified as the third oldest man in the world.

Entrance fee payable. **Open:** daily except for Mondays: 0930-1730, last admission at 1630, (15 Nov-15 Feb: 1300-1700) Tel: + (0) 57 33 32 28. Fax: + (0) 57 33 21 83.
E-mail: info@talbot.house.be Website: www.talbothouse.be Visits for groups must be booked in advance.

Turn right on the R33 and then take the N308 (not the N38) direction Ieper and continue to Brandhoek Church.

Chavasse Memorial. Lat & Long: 50.85470 2.79018.

Beneath the Union flag is a Memorial bearing a photo and brief history of the extraordinary double VC, Capt Noel Chavasse of the Liverpool Scottish Territorials. It was unveiled to commemorate the 80th Anniversary of his death on 29 August 1997. Chavasse, a Medical Officer, was awarded a posthumous Bar to the VC he won on 9/10 August 1916 on the Somme. Both acts of gallantry were for tending the wounded under fire, the second time until he himself was mortally wounded.

Turn down the road opposite, just passed, following CWGC signs to the Brandhoek group of cemeteries, crossing the railway and dual carriageway

(N38). Continue past Brandhoek Military Cemetery on the left and turn right to Brandhoek New Military Cemetery (with Brandhoek New Military Cemetery No 3 opposite on the left). Lat & Long: 50.85242 2.78826.
In Brandhoek New Mil, Lat & Long 50.85242 2.78826, is buried **Capt Noel Godfrey Chavasse, VC and Bar, MC, RAMC.** His full citation from the *London Gazette* may be read in the Cemetery Report.
Return to the N38.

Continue on the N38 and follow signs into the centre of Ieper and park in the Grand' Place (Main Square) in front of the large cathedral-like building (small parking fee from meter).

This is the Cloth Hall. The actual Cathedral (St Martin's) is behind it and there is more parking in front of it. At the eastern end of the Cloth Hall are :

• In Flanders Fields Museum/Regional Visitors' Centre & Shop, Cloth Hall/ Map 1/1. Lat & Long: 50.85128 2.88683

IMPORTANT NOTE. A major redesign of the Museum, Tourist Office, Boutique and offices is planned for the series of 100th Anniversaries which start in 2014. In the meantime part or some of the existing facilities will be closed from time to time, e.g. from 1 Dec 2010-31 Jan 2011; 1 Feb 2011-18 Sept 2011;19 Sept 2011-31 March 2012. **Sunday 1 April 2012** is the target date for **reopening** the renovated museum. The entrance point will change as the redevelopment, which involves many internal structural changes, progresses. Watch out for signs.

The 1998 Museum was named after John McCrae's 1915 poem (qv), emphasising the fact that the Museum extended beyond the confines of the Cloth Hall to the battlefields which surround it. While incorporating some of the invaluable collections of the small but well-loved Salient Museum which it replaced, the Museum made extensive use of the latest state of the art technology and presentation techniques. It explored Ieper's current importance as a 'Town of Peace', comparable to Hiroshima and Stalingrad.

The new 2012 version Museum, costing some €10million, will occupy virtually the entire Cloth Hall (other than new **Caféteria**, the re-housed Documentation Centre, enlarged Tourist Office and Municipal offices). As ever it will have good facilities for disabled visitors, including an elevator.

While still making use of cutting edge technology where appropriate, now that the last human witness, Harry Patch (qv) has died, the Museum will in many respects revert to the eloquent use of artefacts and objects, especially personal and land-related items (such as models of archaeological sites), to give strong evidence of the period. The battlefield surrounding the Museum (now extending to cover the entire area from the Belgian Front to the Lys) plays an increasingly important role in bearing witness to the cataclysmic events of '14-'18. In the Museum, national themes will be emphasised and visitors will log in, giving their nationality and region, so that they can then follow story lines throughout the Museum that relate to their local interest in their own language. The chronological journey starts with the pre-War Belgian home front, followed by a walk across a huge steel plate on the path of the German invasion through Liège to the Marne. Next comes the unfolding story of the War on Belgian soil and the aftermath.

At the centre will be an amazing Belfry Experience. Once again visitors (max 20 at a time, and with a small additional fee) will be able to mount the 205 stairs (with stops to catch breath at several platforms where information will be displayed). At the top those who can get through the very narrow final entrance will be rewarded by stunning views over the region from the Yser Tower to Cassel. Over 1,500 aerial photos will be projected on multi-touch LCD screens which will have the capacity of zooming in on monuments, cemeteries and important sites on the map of the entire front.

Currently visitors to the museum exit through the Regional Visitors' Centre and shop on the ground floor (which also have their own separate entrance on the square.) The Centre describes the attractions of the Westhoek area (Ieper, Poperinge, Heuvelland, Zonnebeke, Wervik, Langemark-Poelkapelle, Mesen and Vleteren). There is an information counter where one can obtain details of accommodation, restaurants and current events. The shop stocks an impressive range of guide books, maps and souvenirs, driving, cycling and walking routes around the battlefields of 'The In Flanders Fields Route' and 'The Ijzer Front Route' and other themed routes.

Battlefield tours may be booked here using official local guides (see page 106).
Current Opening times: 1 April-15 November 1000-1800, every day.16 November-31 March 1000-1700. Closed Mondays, Christmas and New Year's Day and the first three weeks after the Christmas holidays. Ticket sales stop one hour before closing time. Entrance fee payable with special rates for students and groups.
Contact: Cloth Hall, Grote Markt 34, 8900 Ieper. Tel: + (0) 57 23 92 20. Fax: + (0) 57 23 92 75.
E-mail: flandersfields@ieper.be **Website:** www.inflandersfields.be

Leave the museum on foot keeping left via the archway at the corner of the Nieuwerck with the Klein Stadhuis Restaurant and continue left around the building (in which, incidentally, there are good public toilets).

Opposite is St Martin's Cathedral in which there are several WW1 Memorials.
Go past and turn right on Coomansstraat. St George's Church is on the far corner on the opposite side of the road to the cathedral.

• *St George's Memorial Church/Map 1/2/Lat & Long: 50.85237 2.88288*

The idea of having a British memorial church or chapel in Ypres was raised formally as early as 1920 when the Church Army appealed for donations to establish a building fund. In 1924 Sir John French, who had taken the title Earl of Ypres, added his voice to the call and the foundation stone was laid on Sunday, 24 July 1927. On 24 March 1929 the church was dedicated by the Right Reverend Bishop of Fulham. As a tribute to the 342 Old Etonians who fell in the Salient the College provided the 'British School' which is next door to the church. Newly renovated it is now used as the Church Hall and the CWGC staff club house. Services are held every Sunday and on 11 November each year the congregation is swelled by hundreds of people from all over Britain and spills into the nearby theatre or the Cloth Hall.

Every item in the church is a memorial, from the beautiful stained-glass windows to the chairs, on each of which is a brass plate naming the missing loved one. On the south wall of the church is a bust of Sir John French and on either side of it memorials to Field Marshal Montgomery and Sir Winston Churchill who both served in the Salient. New memorials continue to be erected, for the church now commemorates the fallen of both World Wars. A few

minutes contemplation in this home of memory brings gentle pride in the solid beliefs of the men who fought for King and Country and there is sadness too that so many had to suffer, both on the battlefield and left alone at home. It is right to remember the sacrifice and the penalties and here it can be done without pomp or circumstance.

In 2010 the popular and energetic Chaplain for many years, Ray Jones, was replaced by the Revd Brian Llewellyan.
The church is open from 0930 until dusk (1600 hours in the winter) and there are postcards available on a table beside the door, a visitors' book to be signed and a collection box. Tel: + (0) 57 21 56 85.

The colourful kneelers In the Church.

Return to the main square and walk up the Menin (Meensestraat) Road to the Menin Gate.

• The Menin Gate, Indian Memorial, RB Australian Memorial/Map 1/3/Lat & Long: 50.85217 2.89166

Winston Churchill said of Ypres, 'A more sacred place for the British race does not exist in the world', and proposed that the town be left in ruins as an eternal memorial to the million men who fought in the Salient. The townspeople had other ideas and began to rebuild their homes, and it was agreed that on the site of an old Vauban gateway from Ypres on the road to Menin, the road taken by tens of thousands of British soldiers on their way to the trenches, a memorial arch should be constructed. Work under Sir Reginald Blomfield began in 1923. The material used was French limestone and the arch is 80 ft high, 135 ft long and 104 ft wide. It was unveiled on 24 July 1927 by Field Marshal Plumer (the same day that he laid the foundation stone of St George's Church) in the presence of the King of the Belgians and many thousands of veterans and relatives of the Fallen. The whole ceremony was transmitted by wireless by the BBC and the Last Post was sounded at the Gate for the first time. Carved over all the walls of the great gate, inside, up the stairs and around the top on each side overlooking the ramparts are the names of almost 55,000 soldiers who fell in the Salient between the beginning of the war and 15 August 1917. They simply disappeared.

In his address Lord Plumer said, 'It can be said of each one in whose honour we are assembled here today, "He is not missing, he is here".'

Among the 54,000 names recorded on its panels – each important to those who mourn – are the poets **Lt John Collinson Hobson**, MGC, killed on 31 July 1917, **Lt Walter Scott Stuart Lyon** (qv), Royal Scots, killed on 8 May 1915, **Capt the Hon C.E.A. Philipps** (qv), RHG killed on 13 May 1915, and **Lt Gerald George Samuel**, RWK, killed on 7 June 1917.

Also listed are **2nd Lt Henry Anthony Birrell-Anthony**, 1st Bn the Monmouthshire Regt, killed on 8 May 1915, who is mentioned on the Monmouth Memorial at St Julien; **Lt Aidan Chavasse** of the 17th King's Liverpool Regiment, missing in action on 4 July 1917 (youngest brother of Noel Chavasse (qv), the Double VC winner); **Lt the Hon W.A.M. ('Bill') Eden**, KRRC, killed on 3 March 1915, cousin of Anthony Eden (later Prime Minister); **2nd Lt the Hon Gerald William ('Billy') Grenfell**, Rifle Brigade, brother of the poet Julian Grenfell; **Lt Alexis Helmer**, 1st Bde Field Artillery, inspiration for John McCrae's poem *In Flanders Fields*, killed on 2 May 1915; **2nd Lt Arthur Oscar Hornung**, Attd 2nd Bn the Essex Regiment, killed on 6 July 1915, son of E. W. Hornung, creator of Raffles, the 'Gentleman Burglar' and nephew of Conan Doyle; **L/Cpl Thomas ('Pat') Rafferty** of the R Warwicks, Bruce Bairnsfather's inspiration for 'Old Bill'; three men who were executed: **Driver T. Moore**, of 24 Div Train ASC, shot on 26 February 1916, for murder, **Cpl George Povey** of the Cheshire Regt, shot on 11 February 1915, **Pte W Scotton** of the 4th Middlesex, shot on 3 February 1915.

Victoria Cross Winners commemorated are **L/Cpl Frederick Fisher** of the Quebec Regt, killed on 24 April 1915; **Brig-Gen Charles FitzClarence** of the Irish Guards, killed on 12 November 1914 near Polygon Wood commanding the 1st Guards Brigade (a Boer War VC); **Sgt Maj F.W. Hall** of the 8th Manitoba Regt, killed on 25 April 1915; **2nd Lt Dennis George Wyldbore Hewitt** of the 14th Hampshires, killed on 31 July 1917; **Capt John Franks Vallentin**, 1st S Staffs, killed on 7 November 1914; **Pte Edward Warner**, 1st Beds, killed on 2 May 1915, near Hill 60 and **2nd Lt Sidney Woodroffe** of the Rifle Brigade, killed on 30 July 1915, friend of, and subject of a poem by, the poet Charles Sorley (qv).

Pte James Smith of the 1st Bn the Black Watch, killed on 31 October 1914, has the Regimental Number '1'. **Capt A.E.B. O'Neill** of the 2nd Life Guards was the first Member of Parliament (for Mid Antrim) to be killed in the war on 6 November 1914. Brothers-in-law of the 1st Life Guards, **Capt Lord Hugh Grosvenor** (son of the Duke of Westminster) and **Lt the Hon Gerald Ward, MVO** (son of the 1st Earl of Dudley) both disappeared in the fighting of 30 October 1914, at Zantvoorde.

Note that the UK names inscribed on the wall are for the period up to 15 August 1917, after which date they were inscribed on the Memorial Wall at Tyne Cot. The names of Australians, Canadians, Indians and South Africans are for the entire duration of the war: they have no names on the Tyne Cot Memorial. There are no New Zealand names on the wall – they have their own memorials throughout the Salient.

On the town side at the top of the arch is a sarcophagus, while looking down the Menin Road is a British lion sculpted by Sir Reid Dick RA. Under each is an inscription by Kipling (after whom the street to the left beyond the arch is named).

At ground level in the pillars are the bronze boxes containing the Memorial Reports with details of those commemorated, first in regimental order and then by name. The ramparts should be visited above the Gate, access being via the stairways to each side of the centre. To the right on the ramparts is the significant new **Indian Memorial** unveiled on 12 November 2010 (replacing that unveiled in 2002) and to the left is the bronze **Ross Bastiaan** (qv) **Australian Memorial**. It

Poppy tributes at Menin Gate, 11 November.

is possible to walk around the beautifully renovated ramparts to the Lille (Rijsel) Gate.

Return to your car and leave the Square, driving out round the Cloth Hall, turning right up Coomansstraat and left past St George's Church on Elverdingsestraat.

The HQ of the CWGC is on the right at no 82, with flagpoles outside. **Lat & Long: 50.85149 2.87738.** Tel: + (0) 57 22 36 36. Fax: + (0) 57 21 80 14. **E-mail:** neaoffice@cwgc.org

Continue to the first roundabout and turn right signed A19, Veurne. Continue to the next roundabout and turn right on the N379 signed Centrum and turn left at the next roundabout signed Diksmuide on the N369. Continue under the motorway bridge to the British war cemetery on the right with flagpoles. Stop.

• **Essex Farm CWGC Cemetery/Albertina Memorial/Dressing Station/49th (W Riding) Div Memorial/2.3 miles/20 minutes/ Map 1/4, 1/5, 1/6/Lat & Long: 50.87109 2.87276**

Outside the cemetery is an **Albertina Memorial** to the **poet John McCrae** (qv), unveiled on 15 November 1985 by the Governor of West Flanders and executed by the sculptor Pieter-Hein Boudens of Bruges. Unlike the other Albertina Memorials (qv), McCrae's bears a poppy instead of King Albert's Royal Cipher. To the left of the cemetery is a house and behind it some concrete dugouts. Between 1915 and 1917 these were used as a dressing station. Third Ypres casualties from the 51st (Highland) and 38th (Welsh) Divisions were treated here.

Canadian Medical Officer Colonel **John McCrae**, who had served with the Artillery in the Boer War, had written what is perhaps the war's best-known poem, In Flanders Fields, when he served in what was then a simple earthen dugout dressing station in the spring of 1915. On 24 April McCrae wrote home with one of the most vivid and moving accounts of the Second Battle of Ypres. He saw the 'asphyxiated French soldiers' and streams of civilian refugees – 'the very picture of debacle'. By 25 April the Canadians had lost 6,000 of their strength of 10,000. The shelling was unremitting and the small cemetery beside the dressing station grew daily. On 2 May, one of McCrae's patients and a friend, Lt Alexis Helmer, was virtually blown to pieces by a direct hit by an 8in shell. McCrae was touched by the last words in Helmer's diary, 'It has quieted a little and I shall try to get a good sleep'. McCrae said the committal service over Helmer's body. 'A soldier's death,' he commented. A wooden cross was put over Helmer's grave and the Colonel was moved to write his famous lines,

> In Flanders fields the poppies blow
> Between the crosses, row on row,
> That mark our place...

The poem was published in *Punch* on 8 December 1915, and became an instant popular success. From it the symbol of the poppy was taken by the British Legion to represent remembrance of those who gave their lives in the Great War and subsequent conflicts.

Helmer's grave was lost in the subsequent fighting over the ground and he is commemorated on the Menin Gate.

In the early spring of 1995 extensive restoration began in the concrete bunkers of the dressing station at the joint initiative of the Ieper Town Council, Talbot House and local school children. It was completed in time for the

Essex Farm Bunker Dressing Station.

eightieth anniversary of the writing of McCrae's poem on 3 May 1995, when an impressive ceremony was held. Now the various chambers which housed the Officers' Mess, the wards for walking cases and stretcher cases, the latrines, the mess kitchen, the area for the wounded to be evacuated, the stores and offices – all built in 1916/17 – can once again clearly be seen. At the entrance is a **Memorial with bronze Plaques** placed by the Historic Sites & Monuments Board of Canada with a brief summary of McCrae's career and his famous poem.

The sheer volume of visitors to this site was overwhelming it and in spring 2003 extensive landscaping was undertaken, leading visitors on gravel paths to the 49th Div Memorial and to the canal bank 'to spread the load' with Information Boards along the way.

The cemetery contains 1,088 UK, 9 Canadian, 102 Unknown, 5 German prisoners and 19 special memorials. They include **15-year-old Private V.J. Strudwick** of 8th Bn the Rifle Brigade, killed on 14 January 1916, and **Pte Thomas Barratt, VC,** of the 7th Bn the S Staffs Regt who on 27 July 1917, acted as the scout to a successful patrol, killing two German snipers and covering the patrol's withdrawal, but was killed by a shell on his return. Also buried here is **Lt Frederick Leopold Pusch,** DSO, of the 1st Bn Irish Guards, age 20, killed on 27 June 1916. A silver memorial cup, inscribed to Lt Pusch – 'M. H. 19081910', was found by the authors in the shop at Delville Wood Museum on the Somme. His 19-year-old brother, 2nd Lt E. J. Pusch of the 11th Bn the Royal Warwickshires, was killed on 19 August 1916, and is buried in Flatiron Copse CWGC Cemetery on the Somme. **Lt Donald Campbell** of the Coldstream Guards, killed on 19 July 1916, and buried here is the son of Capt the Hon John B Campbell, DSO, age 48, of the same regiment, who had been killed on 25 January 1915, and is commemorated on the Le Touret Memorial.

Behind the cemetery on the canal bank is the **Memorial Column to the 49th (West Riding) Division** inaugurated in 1924. The 49th, a territorial division, came out early in 1915. It had the dubious distinctions of being, together with 6th Division, one of the first to face a phosgene attack when the two divisions suffered over 1,000 casualties from the gas alone and in the winter of 1915 having more than 400 cases of trench foot in just one battalion. Trench foot was the result of prolonged standing in water in flooded trenches. The feet swelled to football-sized proportions and became painfully sensitive to the extent that the sufferer found it virtually impossible to walk and hence became unfit for duty.

Continue on the N6 past the turn off to the village of Boezinge and take the first turning to the right signed Langemark. Continue over the canal and take the third right signed Ieper. Continue 0.7 mile along the canal bank to the left turn on Bargiestraat at the Biovita buildings with flags and follow the road to the left to the site, with a series of huge windmills to the right.

• *Boezinge Archaeological Battlefield Site-Yorkshire Trench/5.5 miles/15 minutes/Map 1/7/Lat & Long: 50.88833 2.87431*

This is the site, first explored by the 'Diggers' (an amateur archaeology group, qv) in February 1992 of an important trench and dugout system known as Yorkshire Trench. The incredibly well-preserved 'A' frames and other original elements discovered in the retentive Flanders blue clay mud have been incorporated in a representation of the system in the In Flanders Fields Museum. At the site itself the Town of Ieper have recreated the trench and entrance to the dugout, with realistic looking sandbags and duckboards, with several explanatory panels, inaugurated in May 2003.

Turn round and return to the Langemark-Poelkapelle road and turn right on Langemarkseweg.

You are now travelling along the Pilckem Ridge. At 7.0 miles **Artillery Wood CWGC Cemetery** (where the poets 'Hedd Wyn' and Francis Ledwidge are buried) is signed to the left and the Irish flag which flies over the Ledwidge Memorial can be seen. On the corner is the **Breton Memorial (Map 1/8, Lat & Long: 50.89720 2.87433)**.

Continue another 1.3 miles.

On the house on the right just before the crossroads (Iron Cross) where Ruisseau Farm CWGC Cemetery is signed to the left are **Plaques to the poet 'Hedd Wyn'** (Ellis Humphrey Evans), **Map 1/9, Lat & Long: 50.90328 2.90097**. Contact the owners of the Liva Banquet Hall opposite for plans for more Hedd Wyn activities including a monthly ceremony: liva.lorenzo@skynet.be

Continue a further 0 .2 miles passing **Cement House CWGC Cem** on the right **(Map C14, Lat & Long: 50.9050 2.90700)**

Continue a further 0.8 mile keeping right at the left hand bend.

[N.B. At this point by turning left and then turning right along a track (just before the '100m/Cycle Path/Bend' sign) a small flat, rather difficult to spot, **Memorial to Harry Patch** (qv) may be seen to the left on the bank of the Steenbeek. **Lat & Long: 50.90979 2.90864.]**

On crossing the Steenbeek, on the bridge to the left is an **Albertina Memorial (Map 1/11, Lat & Long: 50.90746 2.91365)** to mark the end of the Steenbeek Offensive.

Just beyond, on the left is the tall

20th Light Division Memorial (Map 1/12, Lat & Long: 50.90836 2.91564).

Continue to the Langemark crossroads/traffic lights. Turn left (the 'no left turn' restriction only applies to heavy vehicles) and follow signs to Diksmuide and

'Deutsche Soldaten Friedhof'. Park in the parking area of the Interpretative Centre beyond the cemetery and to the left.

• Langemarck German Cemetery & Interpretative Centre/10.1 miles/35 minutes/Map 1/13/WC/Lat & Long: 50.92164 2.91675

In June 2006 a new **Interpretative Centre** and parking area was opened on the land adjoining the cemetery to the north - a joint initiative of West Flanders, the Commune of Langemarck and the *Kriegsgräbefürsorge*. In it there are maps, photos and documentation and 3 video screens briefly explaining a) The First Battle of Ypres; b) The Gas Attack of April 1915; c) The history of the cemetery and the work of the *Kriegsgräbefürsorge*. Sadly there were no German veterans present at the unveiling. The last German WW1 veteran, Charles Kuentz, who fought in Ypres, on the Somme and on the Eastern front, died in April 2005, aged 108. In 2004 he made a pilgrimage to Passchendaele where he met the British veteran, Harry Patch (qv), then 106. Gaymer's Cider produced a special 'Patch's Pride' brew in his honour.

The Cemetery is now approached by passing through the building and walking along the Cemetery wall to the main entrance.

This area was captured by the British 20th (Light) Division on 16 August during the Third Ypres offensive of 1917. It had been defended by the French in 1914 and lost on 22 April 1915 (Second Ypres) during the gas attack. In continuing operations in October 1917 the 4th Bn Worcester Regiment were ordered to push further north from here. On the evening of 7 October the battalion had marched out from Ypres following the route you have driven, turned right at Boezinghe and along the Pilckem Ridge via duckboards to the front line at the northern end of the cemetery. They were in position by dawn on 8 October and spent the day preparing for their assault. In the engagement that followed the next day a famous **VC** was won by **Private Frederick George Dancox** (qv), a solid old soldier who captured a nearby pillbox (qv).

The Cemetery is maintained by the *Volksbund Deutsche Kriegsgräberfürsorge* – the German People's Organisation for the Care of War Graves – and is the only German cemetery in the actual Salient. When the war was over the German dead were all amalgamated into four cemeteries – Langemarck, Menin, Vladslo and Hooglede. As the bodies were exhumed, all those that could be identified were reburied in marked graves, sometimes several inscribed on one tombstone to symbolize comradeship in death. The unknowns were buried in a mass grave. Most of the landscaping work was completed between 1970 and 1972, much of it by international students working voluntarily during their vacations, although detailed work at Langemarck was not completed until the late 1980s.

Langemarck is one of the largest German cemeteries in Belgium, with 44,292 bodies, and has an impressive entrance with two chambers, one with the names of the missing carved in oak, and the other bearing a relief map showing the past and present German cemeteries in Belgium and containing the Visitors' book and Cemetery Register. The cemetery is planted with oak trees, the symbol of German strength, and in the communal grave rest the remains of 25,000 soldiers – half of whose names are known. The four impressive sculptures which overlook the cemetery were executed by Professor Emil Krieger and around the mass grave are the Regimental insignia of the student brigades who fought in this area. In the north wall of the cemetery are the remains of some massive German block-houses, doubtless similar to the one that Private Dancox captured.

In December 2004 a small bronze **Plaque** was attached to the end of the left hand column surrounding the mass grave. It commemorates **Pte A. Carlill**, Loyal North Lancs, 4 November 1918 and **Pte L.H. Lockley,** Seaforth Highlanders, 30 October 1918, both now known to be buried in the mass grave. Their names were located on the bronze panels (to be found by searching alphabetically, noting that Lockley is listed as 'Lookley') by researchers Michel Vansuyt and Michel Van den Bogaert. Carlill, sometimes recorded as 'Carhill' was originally recorded by the CWGC as being buried in Louvain Communal Cemetery, German Plot, and listed on the Loos Memorial, while Lockley was listed in Jemappes Communal Cemetery.

Langemarck Cemetery was on the route of Adolf Hitler's June 1940 tour of the Salient.

Plaque to Ptes Carlill and Lockley, German Cemetery, Langemarck.

[**N.B. 1.** By turning left out of the car park, and taking the first turning left along Beekstraat a **Bunker** and **the Memorial to 34th Division, RE and RA (Lat & Long: 50.92420 2.91335)** may be reached.

N.B. 2. By turning left out of the car park and driving some .7 mile to the small turning to the right along Galgestraat and continuing some .6 mile, past a house on the right to the cycle path (along the disused railway line), a small **Memorial to Pte Dancox VC** which was unveiled in September 2006 near the pillbox he took **(Lat & Long: 50.92754 2.93616)** may be reached.]

Drive back to Langemarck traffic lights and continue straight over, signed Ieper to the next crossroads with the N313. Continue straight over to the crossroads where there is a tall memorial column opposite.

[**N.B.** By turning left out here and driving some 1.5 miles into Poelkapelle to the roundabout in the centre is the **Memorial to WW1 French aviator Guynemer,** CO of the *Cigogne* (Stork) Squadron and France's most popular 'Ace', with 54 kills. His plane was brought down near Poelkapelle on 11 September 1917). By the parking area just beyond it on the right is the new **Tank Memorial (Lat & Long: 50.91767 2.95708)**. Sponsored by Chris Lock and his wife Milena, it is on the site of the old 'Tank Cemetery' and was inaugurated on 10 October 2009. A register Box contains a Visitor's Book and folder full of interesting information (for more details see www.tankmemorial.vpweb.co.uk).]

Cross over and stop in the car park on the left.

• The Brooding Soldier, Vancouver Corner/12.1 miles/10 minutes/Map 1/14/Lat & Long: 50.89916 2.94044.

This remarkable, dramatic Memorial, represents a soldier standing with 'arms reversed', the traditional stance at a funeral. When the Canadian government decided to erect memorials in Europe to their war dead they initiated a competition to find the most appropriate design. This was the runner-up. The winning design was erected on Vimy Ridge. The architect here was Chapman Clemesha, from Regina, who had fought in the war and had been wounded. The 35-ft high central column of Vosges stone rises out of a circular pavement on which are marked direction indicators to other parts of the battlefield. The bowed helmeted head was carved in Brussels. At the back of the memorial is the bronze box containing the visitors' book. The inscription on the column in French and in English reads. 'This column marks the battlefield where 18,000 Canadians on the British left withstood the first German gas attacks the 22nd-24th April 1915. Two thousand fell and lie here buried.' 'Here buried' does not literally mean on this spot, but over the battlefield. The memorial was unveiled on 8 July 1912 by the Duke of Connaught in the presence of Marshal Foch. The Canadian cedars are trimmed to represent shells.

The German gas attack launched in the afternoon of 22 April 1915 caught the Allies by surprise. The French Colonial troops on the left side of the allied line broke before the gas and the Canadians, with British county regiment reinforcements – the Buffs, Middlesex, York and Lancs, Leicesters – moved into the gap and held both that attack and the second on 25 April. The soldiers had no gas masks but discovered that, by soaking handkerchiefs in water and stuffing them into their mouths, they could get some relief. This road junction is also known as Vancouver Corner and Kerselaar.

[N.B. On the wall of the red brick building opposite is a **Plaque to Lt Edward Donald Bellew VC**, 7th Bn CEF, who won his VC near this site. It was unveiled on 8 September 2008.]

Continue past the Brooding Soldier towards Zonnebeke. After some 200m take the small road, Vrouwstraat, to the left, past the glasshouses. This leads to the mill.

• Totemuhle (Death Mill)/12.5 miles/Lat & Long: 50.89740 2.94828

The original mill on this site earned its title during its use by the Germans as an observation post. In such flat countryside even a few metres of additional height greatly increased visibility and Forward Observation Officers directing artillery fire often carried their own step ladders to climb upon. When you are sitting in a coach you are roughly at the height of a man on horseback.

Near the Totemuhle served Erich Maria Remarque, author of the German classic *All Quiet on the Western Front*. The mill may be visited and opening times are posted outside.

Continue to the right of the mill. Pass a small junction to the left and stop just before the next junction to the right opposite a calvary.

• Observation Point/12.8 miles/5 minutes/OP *(crops permitting)*/Lat & Long: 50.89460 2.95418

You are in the middle of the battlefields of Second and Third Ypres. Take 12 o'clock to be your direction of travel. At 10 o'clock is the rectangular shape of Passchendaele water tower and at 11 o'clock the spire of Passchendaele Church. The Passchendaele-Messines Ridge runs from 11 o'clock to 2 o'clock. The tall chimneys at Zonnebeke are at 1 o'clock. The bulk of Kemmel Hill may be seen on the horizon just to the left of Ypres which is at 3 o'clock, with the other Flanders hills behind it and Langemarck Church can be seen past the mill at 6 o'clock. On a clear day the tops of a group of four poplars may be seen between 11 and 12 o'clock through the buildings beyond the near horizon. That is Tyne Cot Cemetery. Before the beginning of Second Ypres the Germans held the ridge, the British the area you can see between Ypres and some 3km to your left.

Aerial view of Tyne Cot Cemetery.

*New Zealand Memorial,
s-Graventafel.*

*The Brooding
Soldier.*

Following the success of the chlorine gas on 22 April 1915, the Germans released their next cloud at 0400 hours on 24 April in the area to your left. It swept across the road on which you are now standing, while German artillery kept up a continuous assault on British positions in the Salient. The German forces involved here were part of the 51st Reserve Division and, in particular, the 4th Marine Brigade which advanced through here on the following day. **Map 2** page 26 shows the extent of the German advance when the assault ended on 25 May. At the beginning of Third Ypres in June 1917 this spot was just to the rear of the German third main trench line.

Continue along the road to a Memorial on the left.

• Memorial to 15th Bn, 48th Highlanders of Canada/13.3 miles/5 minutes/Lat & Long: 50.89303 2.96507

On a clear bronze Plaque with badge the Memorial tells the story of the 22 April 1915 gas attack (the first major engagement of 1 Can Div) in considerable detail. It was inaugurated on 24 April 2010.

Continue to the next crossroads.

• s-Graventafel Crossroads, New Zealand Memorial/14 miles/10 minutes/Map 1/15/Lat & Long: 50.89067 2.97855

The column on the left commemorates the men of the New Zealand Division in the battle of Broodseinde of 4 October 1917. On a front extending from around Geluveld (roughly 5 miles south of here) to just short of Houthulst (some 6 miles north of here), an attack began at 0600 on 4 October in which Australian, New Zealand and English divisions took part. By chance the attack went in 10 minutes before the Germans planned to launch their own assault and the Germans thus suffered severely from artillery fire, much of the fighting then being finished off with the bayonet. The task of taking the Zonnebeke/s-Graventafel spur was given to the 2nd Anzac Corps and the stiffest opposition was faced in this area which was taken by the New Zealanders under Maj-Gen Sir A.H. Russell. By the end of the day the division had taken over 1,100 prisoners and 59 machine guns.

Continue straight over the crossroads onto Schipstraat (now prohibited to buses which should follow signs to the left here). Continue and turn left along Vijfwegenstraat, and then follow signs (past the original entry to the cemetery where there is now no parking) to the right to the parking area behind the cemetery.

• Tyne Cot CWGC Cemetery, New Zealand, Sherwood Foresters & KOYLI Memorials, Interpretative Centre/15.1 miles/30 minutes/Map 1/16/Lat & Long: 50.88771 3.00113

On this forward slope of the Passchendaele Ridge are both the largest British war cemetery in the world and a Memorial Wall designed by Sir Herbert Baker on which are commemorated the almost 35,000 UK soldiers missing with no known grave for whom room could not be found on the Menin Gate, i.e. those killed after 15 August 1917. In the centre is the New Zealand Memorial, listing 1,176 names (in line with their decision to have their own separate national memorials). All other Commonwealth Missing are on the Menin Gate.

On the Ridge German pillboxes were erected and inside the cemetery on each side of the central path two of them can still be seen, now surrounded by poplar trees and at the end of the path is the Cross of Sacrifice which has been built on top of a third pillbox. In 1922 King George V and Queen Mary toured the battlefields and, 'Tyne Cot he saw for the first time this May afternoon. He understood how appalling was the task that his soldiers faced there and turning to the great pillbox which still stands in the middle of the cemetery he said that it should never be moved, it should always remain as a monument to the heroes whose graves stood thickly around. From its roof he gazed sadly over the sea of wooden crosses, a 'massed multitude of silent witnesses to the desolation of war'. It is indeed fitting that this should form, as it will, the foundation for the great Cross of Sacrifice shortly to be built up as a central memorial in this cemetery.' (The King's Pilgrimage, Rudyard Kipling)

Today at the base of the cross a small patch of that original block-house can still be seen, contained within a bronze wreath, while on the far side of the cross, between it and the memorial wall, is a higgledy piggledy collection of some 300 graves. These are the original battle burials left where they were found after the Armistice. They included some German graves. The other, almost 12,000, graves which stand in parade ground order, were brought in from all the surrounding area. The majority of them are unidentified. The report for the cemetery is in a box under the entrance porch and the reports for the memorial wall are in the left-hand loggia. It is a sobering experience to look for one's own name in the reports and many a visitor has discovered the details of an unknown relative.

Looking back from the cross to the entrance, the chimneys of Zonnebeke should be visible well to the left and to their right on the near horizon the spires of the Cloth Hall can be seen on a clear day. The battle of Third Ypres surged up to here for three months from the direction of Ypres, the Germans holding this ridge, defending it with pill-boxes, machine guns, barbed wire and mustard gas. It was an Empire battle, the graves bearing witness to the team effort – some 8,900 from the UK, 1,350 from Australia, almost 1,000 from Canada and over 500 from New Zealand.

It was not until the end of October 1917 that the village and the ridge were taken, much of the latter in this area by the Australians and the empty village by the Canadians. In an action on 12 October the Australian 34th Infantry Battalion attacked two German pillboxes 400 yards north of here and was held down by heavy machine-gun fire. **Captain Clarence Jeffries** organised and led a bombing party against the pillbox on the right, taking 35 prisoners and capturing four machine guns. He then led a successful attack on another machine-gun emplacement and while attempting yet another he was killed. Born in Wallsend, New South Wales on 26 October 1894, Jeffries joined the militia at the age of fourteen, and was promoted to Captain four months before his death in the action which won him the **VC**. He and five other **VCs** are buried or commemorated here, including **Sgt Lewis McGee**, of the 40th AIF, who was killed taking a pillbox at nearby Hamburg Farm. This is truly a 'Silent City', each headstone representing not just a life lost, but a family bereaved and generations unborn. Standing beside the white sentinels on this now peaceful hillside in Flanders, it is difficult to believe that all the suffering was worthwhile – and yet, simply to be able to stand here is a privilege won and paid for by many thousands who lost everything they had, including their name, and whose headstone reads only 'A Soldier of the Great War Known Unto God' – a phrase chosen by Kipling.

On the 90th Anniversary of the Battle in July 2006 an unmanned **Interpretative Centre** with panoramic views over the battlefields, a large car park and toilet facilities (you will need 50 cents) were inaugurated by HM Queen Elizabeth, as was a **Memorial to the KOYLI**. This is now joined by a **Sherwood Foresters (Notts & Derby Regt) Memorial,** the first WW1 Memorial to the Regiment in France or Belgium. Made of Derbyshire stone it was inaugurated on 24 October 2009. Sadly the memorial stones have not weathered well. These were all constructed behind the cemetery so as not to obstruct the fine vista of the approach and a path leads from the Centre round the beautiful flint wall to the front entrance. Funding of 1.5 million Euros was provided for the project by the EC, the Flemish Government, the Province of West Flanders, the Commune of Zonnebeke and a private partner. In the spirit of commemoration of the different nations involved, Information Panels and videos describe the history and construction of the cemetery and illustrate the story of the Battle through the men who took part in it. A huge research project was to make an 'inventory' of as many of the Tyne Cot burials as possible (by pursuing partial identifications, locating original burial sites etc). This has been the dedicated and painstaking task of Belgian WFA Vice-Chairman, Frans Descamps, over many months.

There is now a memorial walk tracing the path of the Australian attack of 4 October 1917 which links the cemetery with the Zonnebeke Museum via the old railway line. Six points along the track have been excavated and in the summer of 2005 the well-preserved body of a soldier of the Lancashire Fusiliers was found, complete with a Flemish Bible, wrist watch, silver cigarette box, wallet containing documents etc. Attempts to make an identification were unsuccessful and eventually the soldier was buried in Tyne Cot Cemetery. The remains of 3 concrete bunkers and some 30 metres of original track were also unearthed. An interesting programme enables students to don WW1 uniform and assume the identity of a soldier buried in Tyne Cot Cemetery. They then walk the old railway route with its well-researched Information Plaques and find 'their' name in the cemetery (apply to the Passchendaele Museum).

Exit the car park following signs to Passchendaele Memorial Museum to the junction with Passendalestraat and turn right. Continue to the next roundabout and turn right on the N332 to Zonnebeke.

The French Memorial is passed on the left, **Lat & Long: 50.87563 3.00172.**

Continue into Zonnebeke.

Zonnebeke. German recce patrols were sighted in this area as early as the last week of August 1914, followed by a large contingent of regular troops in preparation for the First Battle of Ypres on 19 October. From the Second Battle of Ypres in April 1915 the area remained under German occupation until the British Offensive of July 1917 and the dreadful Passchendaele campaign. During the German offensive of spring 1918 the Allies were forced to withdraw towards Ypres until the final offensive of September 1918 when the village was liberated by British and Belgian forces. The Commune of Zonnebeke was completely destroyed during the war but the determined inhabitants returned and the five shattered villages in the area were rebuilt. On the church wall is a **Plaque to the Canadian D21 Bty Field Arty Coy, Lat & Long: 50.87292 2.98804.**

Continue past the church on the left to the Museum with flagpoles on the left. Park on the right (note that there is coach parking and WCs round the corner to the left). Walk through the attractive Château grounds past the Restaurant (closed Mon, Tues) to the Museum entrance.

• *Passchendaele Memorial Museum/Tourist Office, Zonnebeke/16.9 miles/30 minutes/Map 1/17/WC/Lat & Long: 50.87207 2.98683*

On 23 April 2004 a completely new Museum was opened in the lovely 1924 Château. Currently one enters into a small tourist office and book/souvenir stall. To the right and left interesting temporary exhibitions are housed. Upstairs are the fine permanent exhibitions with dioramas, ephemera, photographs, uniforms, weapons, artefacts, gas masks etc interspersed with videos in 4 languages. The visitor is then led down to a trench/dugout/tunnel system, complete with realistic dioramas (e.g. first aid). This is an extremely interesting museum, with sensitive use of modern technology - well worth a visit. **Open:** 1 February-30 November, Mon-Fri: 1000-1800. Groups any time by appointment.

Gasmasks display, Passchendaele Museum.

Entrance fee payable. Tel: + (0) 51 77 04 41.
E-mail: info@passchendaele.be Website:
www.passchendaele.be
N.B. Closing times may change from late
2010 onwards due to work on the large
extension, which is due to open on 1 April
2012. The €2million building will extend
underground into the Chateau park,
doubling the Dugout Experience space. A

Memorial to Australian 5th Div, Polygon Wood.

running presentation of the battle on a huge model of 1917 Passchendale will
feature the landscape (subterranean structures, cemeteries etc) using aerial
photos and a 'National' section will feature the contribution of the Australian,
Canadian, English, Irish, New Zealand, Scots, Welsh etc, with rare wartime film
footage and testimony of last veterans; important Artillery and Engineer sections;

Entrance to the Passchendaele Memorial Museum, Zonnebeke.

a new Trench Experience and a Remembrance section, from 1919 to Today. A thorough visit, with a 400metre walk will take about 2 hours, with a simpler disabled circuit available.

Continue to the second turn to the left and follow signs to Buttes New & Polygon Wood Cemeteries.

• Polygon Wood CWGC Cemetery/Buttes New British CWGC Cemetery/NZ Memorial/Australian 5th Div Memorial/18.3 miles/ 25 minutes/Map 1/18, 1/19, 1/20/Lat & Long:50.85703 2.99089

This area is 1½ miles due north of Gheluvelt (the next stop but one on the itinerary) where the Worcesters distinguished themselves in 1914. You are at the north-eastern end of the wood which in November 1914 (First Ypres) was held by 1st King's Liverpool with just 450 men and 6 officers strung along the 1 mile long southern edge and two companies of the Black Watch in the south-west corner.

On 11 November 1914, the Prussian Guard made a determined attack in massed strength along the axis of the Menin Road moving east to west (see next stop). Their efforts to break through this wood were stopped by dogged resistance by the Kings and the Black Watch. By the end of the day only one Black Watch officer was unwounded. His name was Captain Fortune! The 1st Kings had originally entered the wood during the first week in November and were told to hold it at all costs. They came under shell-fire almost immediately and that, combined with heavy rain, turned the ground into a quagmire. Trenches, such as they were, were knee deep in water and it was impossible to get warm because a fire straightaway brought down German artillery. Hand pumps were used both to draw water and to clear the trenches. Yet, despite their discomfort, the casualties which mounted steadily and being outnumbered, the Kings held on to the wood. Following the German gains made after the gas attacks of April 1915 (Second Ypres) the wood was evacuated and the Germans constructed a number of pillboxes in it as well as tunnelling into the high mound of the old musketry butte.

During 3rd Ypres the wood again featured in a named battle – the 'Battle of Polygon Wood', 26 September to 3 October 1917. The offensive opened at 0550 on 26 September being a rolling barrage with seven divisions in line on a 6-mile front. In the centre were the Australian 4th and 5th Divisions attacking west to east. The wood here and the butte were the objectives of the 14th Australian Brigade, the Australian line stretching north from here to Zonnebeke (from where you have just come).

The barrage was overwhelming. Immediately behind the Australians were the 2nd RWF and Private Frank Richards recalled the experience: 'I entered one pillbox during the day and found 18 dead Germans inside. There was not a mark on one of them. One of our heavy shells had made a direct hit on top of it and they were killed by concussion, but very little damage had been done to the pillbox'. By the end of the day the wood was taken but the two Australian divisions had 5,500 casualties. On top of the butte (which has Information Boards at the base) is a **Memorial to the Australian 5th Division** and below are over 2,000 headstones of the Butte cemetery. This was made after the Armistice by concentrating graves from the Zonnebeke area, almost all of them from 1917. More than four-fifths are unknown, a testimony to the savagery of the fighting. At the far end of the cemetery is a **Memorial to the officers and men of New Zealand** who fell in this area and have no known graves. It has its own register. It was designed by Charles Holden in his distinctive somewhat severe style.

The small cemetery opposite Buttes is **Polygon Wood Cemetery**, begun in August 1917 in the front line, which has some 100 burials, mostly of New Zealanders. There was at one time a German cemetery at the back of it, but the graves have been moved, probably to Langemarck.

Continue along the side of the wood.

On the right at the end is the **Café De Dreve**, owned by archaeologist Johan Vandewalle (qv). Tel: + 57 46 62 35.

Turn left on Lotegatsestraat. Continue until you reach the road bridge over the motorway. Turn left and immediately stop by the gate into the wood.

• **Black Watch Corner/19.3 miles/5 minutes/Map 1/21/OP** *(dependent on foliage/crops!)***/Lat & Long: 50.84850 2.98175**

On 11 November 1914 began the battle known as 'Nonne Boschen' – Nun's Wood. Polygon Wood was at the northen edge of the German attack. Crown Prince Rupprecht ordered the Prussian Guard to take Polygon in co-operation with the 54th Reserve Division. Just after 0630 the German guns opened fire and at 0900 the assault began on a nine-mile front in mist and rain. The barrage had reduced the woods to a tangle of broken trees and undergrowth which impeded the German advance. On almost all of the front the attack faltered but at the southern end of Polygon Wood, between it and Nonne Boschen (where the motorway now is) was a gap in the British line for which the German 3rd Foot Guard Regiment headed. At this south-west corner of the wood, the 23rd Field Company RE under Major C. Russell-Brown had completed a strong point just an hour before the assault, and in it were forty men of the Black Watch commanded by Lt F. Anderson. The position consisted only of a trench inside the hedges of a cottage garden and a few strands of barbed wire but it provided shelter from the artillery. Anderson's party opened such an effective fire on the Guards that they broke formation and were eventually stopped and beaten back by the guns of 2nd Division. In recognition of the role that the Black Watch played here the corner was named after them. It was during this period of fighting that **Captain Brodie** (who has a Private Memorial in Nonne Boschen) of the Cameron Highlanders was killed.

The Brigade formation which had taken the brunt of the attack was the 1st (Guards) Brigade under Brigadier-General FitzClarence (qv) and, having stopped the German assault on 11 November, the Brigadier decided to mount a counter-attack to recover trenches lost to the Germans. While reconnoitring forward of Black Watch Corner he was killed

OP. Stand with your back to the gateway to the corner of the wood and look left along the motorway. Immediately behind the line of trees crossing your front ahead is the village of Geluveld, one mile away. It was from this corner, on 31 October 1914, at the height of the crisis of First Ypres, that Major Hankey led off the 2nd Worcesters in an advance that would end in their famous bayonet charge into the grounds of the château. It was the church spire of Geluveld (Gheluvelt in 1914) that they used as their marker for their objective. (See the next stop).

Continue on Oude Kortrijkstraat to the memorial on the right.

• Memorial to New Zealander Sgt H.J.Nicholas, VC, MM, 1891-1918/22.2 miles/5 minutes/ Lat & Long: 50. 84841 2.99427

The Memorial, unveiled on 14 September 2008, is near the site of the pillbox taken by the then Pte Nicholas, 1st Bn Canterbury Regt.

Continue to the first crossroads then turn right on Reutelhoekstraat. Continue to the T junction, turn left and at the next T junction turn right over the motorway.

As you drive uphill after the bridge you are skirting Geluveld Château and its grounds on the right.

Continue to the church on the right and stop in the car park.

Behind the church and in front of the Château gates is an **Information Board**.

Walk along the path towards the memorials to the left across the road.

• Gheluvelt Mill/Memorials to S Wales Borderers & 2nd Worcesters/22.5 miles/10 minutes/Map 1/22/Lat & Long: 50.83455 2.99447

At the foot of the site of the windmill are Memorials to the 1st South Wales Borderers and to the 2nd Bn Worcestershire Regiment (see illus page 22) which commemorate a famous action of 31 October 1914. The German attacks astride the Menin Road towards Ypres began on 29 October 1914, urged on by the Kaiser, certain that he would soon address his victorious army from the Cloth Hall in Ypres. The German Order of the Day read, 'The break through will be of decisive importance. We must, and therefore will, conquer, settle for ever the centuries long struggle, end the war, and strike the decisive blow against our most detested enemy. We will finish with the British, Indians, Canadians, Moroccans and other trash, feeble adversaries who surrender in mass if they are attacked with vigour.'

The Germans, in overwhelming strength, pushed hard against the thin line of defenders. This area was the responsibility of the British 1st Division under General Lomax (qv). At midday on 31 October Gheluvelt fell and shortly afterwards Lomax was killed by a shell in his headquarters at Hooge (nearer to Ypres). The game was in the balance. General Haig, the Corps Commander, was somewhere along the Menin Road at this time, but unaware of the true tactical situation. However, he did issue orders to the effect that if his Corps could not hold on where it was, it should fall back to a line just in front of Ypres. Meanwhile local commanders took matters into their own hands. The commander of the Menin Road front was **Brigadier-General C. FitzClarence** (qv), late of the Irish Guards, who had won a **VC** as a Captain in the Boer War at Mafeking for 'extraordinary spirit and fearlessness'.

A counter-attack by the 1st South Wales Borderers had made the Germans pause just past Gheluvelt and at 1300 on 31 October FitzClarence called upon the Worcesters, gathered at the southern end of Polygon Wood, to regain the village. The Worcesters were actually part of 2nd Division, but General Lomax had arranged that in an emergency they could be detached to 1st Division. They had been in continuous action for ten days and were down to about 500 men, little more than half of their original strength. Major Hankey, commanding the Worcesters, sent one company to cover the Menin Road itself, lined up his three remaining companies side by side, fixed bayonets and doubled across the open ground between Polygon and the village. Just short of the village was Gheluvelt Château and here the Worcesters found gallant remnants of the South Wales Borderers still hanging on.

Together they pushed forward to the village, now burning furiously and under bombardment from both German and British artillery. Brigadier FitzClarence decided to withdraw to a firmer position and at 1800 the Worcesters and Borders began a move backward to Veldhoek, just under a mile from here along the Menin Road). The German tide had been stopped, but it had cost the Worcesters dear – 187 of the 500 had been killed or wounded. The chase across the open field with bayonets may have saved Ypres, may have saved the BEF, may have saved the war. The British Commander-in-Chief, Sir John French, said that the moment of the counter-attack was 'the worst half-hour of my life'. Sadly, on 12

November, less than two weeks later, Brigadier FitzClarence was killed. His body was never found and he is commemorated on the Menin Gate.

Drive to the crossroads on the main road. Turn right towards Ypres. You are now on the Menin Road. Continue to a crest with a garage complex on the right and the turning to Pappotstraat on the left.

• Clapham Junction/Gloucestershire Memorial/18th Division Memorial/23.7 miles/10 minutes/Map 1/23, 1/24/Lat & Long: 50.84347 2.96192

This was a meeting point for roads and tracks, hence its name. The 1st Battalion of the Gloucestershires saw heavy fighting here during First Ypres and the 2nd Battalion during Second Ypres. Their memorial obelisk is on the right. Opposite on the left is a similar one for the 18th (Eastern) Division which has others in Trones Wood and Thiepval on the Somme.

To the left is the area known as Stirling Castle, named by the Argyll & Sutherland Highlanders after their garrison town and described in 1917 by Col Seton Hutchison in his book Pilgrimage as a 'treacherous heap of filth'.

Continue downhill along the Menin Road, to the memorial by the entrance to the car park for Bellewaerde Leisure Park on the right.

• KRRC Memorial/24.3 miles/5 minutes/Map 1/25/Lat & Long: 50.84575 2.94966

The memorial, which is similar to one on the Somme at Pozières and another in Winchester, is placed here in acknowledgement of the Regiment's part in the battle of 30/31 July 1915 at Hooge Château (qv) and the later battle of Sanctuary Wood (qv) on 2 June 1916. During the war the Regiment grew to twenty-two Battalions.

• Site of Hooge Château/Crater

The leisure park is on the site of the original Château whose destruction began on 31 October 1914, when a shell fell on Maj-Gen Monro's Divisional Headquarters and several staff officers were killed. Others were wounded, including Gen Monro (qv) and Lt-Gen Samuel Holt Lomax (qv), CB, of 1st Division, age 59, who was mortally wounded and eventually died on 10 April 1915. He is buried in the Aldershot Military Cemetery. Several of the casualties are buried in Ypres Town CWGC Cemetery. The crater itself was filled in during the 1920s. It was formed by a mine sprung by 3rd Division on 19 July 1915. The gallery leading to the charge of 3,500lb of ammonal was 190ft long and was prepared by 175th Tunnelling Company RE. When new the crater measured 120ft across and 20ft deep. (For those who know the Lochnagar crater on the Somme, that took 60,000 lbs of ammonal.)

Continue to the Hotel Kasteel to the right and drive into the car park.

• Front Line Hooghe Crater/Preserved Trenches/Bunkers/24.4 miles/15 minutes/RWC/Map 1/26/Lat & Long: 50.84639 2.94624

Beside the hotel, three adjoining water-filled craters (blown by the Germans in June 1916 during the attack on Mount Sorrel) and blockhouses, both in and out of the water, have been excavated and may be visited. There is a box by the entrance of the site for donations to its maintenance. The area where the path runs between the craters and the fenced border of the theme park is where in a surprise attack at 0315 on 30 July 1915, the Germans are said to have first used the flame thrower against British troops. At that time the crater and its immediate surroundings were held by the 8th Rifle Brigade and the 7th Bn KRRC, and jets of flame were sent against both sides of the crater from the direction of today's theme park. The Flammenwerfer equipment that the Germans used was carried by one man and looked rather like a portable fire extinguisher. The liquid was ignited at the nozzle and produced a jet of flame some 25yd long accompanied by thick black smoke.

Both battalions were forced back beyond what is now the rear wall of Hooge Crater Cemetery. Despite further flame attacks that night the line was stabilised some 200yd beyond the other side of the Menin Road and in the two days of fighting the 7th KRRC lost 12 officers and 289 other ranks and 8th Rifle Brigade 19 officers and 462 other ranks.

Bitter fighting had taken place earlier in this sector in 'The Battle of Hooge' (or Belle waerde) of 16/17 June 1915, and the Royal Fusiliers, the Royal Scots Fusiliers and the Northumberland Fusiliers, followed by the Lincolns and the Liverpool Scottish, assaulted enemy trenches between the Menin Road and the Ypers-Roulers railway line. An account of this action, which practically wiped out the Liverpool Scottish, appears in Ann Clayton's biography of **Noel Chavasse** (qv). For it was here that their Medical Officer, who was to go on to win the **VC and Bar**, won the **MC** for 'untiring efforts in personally searching the ground between our line and the enemy's [for which] many of the wounded owe their lives'.

This area is noted for another innovation. It is said that here the first experimental use of portable wireless was attempted between division and brigade HQ. It is to be hoped that the army radios worked better then than they seemed to do at Arnhem in 1944 or even in 21st Century conflicts such as in the Gulf.

The adjoining **Hotel Kasteelhof 't Hooghe and Restaurant**, Tel: + (0) 57 46 87 82, e-mail: kasteelhof.thooghe@belgacom.net website: www.hotelkasteel hofthooghe.be owned and run by the Loontjens family offers not the usual 'sea views' but 'crater views'!

Continue to the Hooge Crater Museum on the right.

Memorioal to 1st Gloucesters, Clapham Junction

Exterior of the Hooge Crater Museum.

One of the Hooghe Craters.

Superb SGW, Hooge Crater Museum.

• *Hooge Crater Museum/24.5 miles/20 minutes/RWC/Map 1/27/Lat & Long:*
50.84634 2.94338

This is truly an atmospheric, traditional, enjoyable, classic style museum. It is housed in the old Chapel at Hooge, built as a memorial to those who fell in the Salient, and was acquired by Roger de Smul, who after extensive renovation, opened it as a museum at Easter 1994. In it he set up two superb private collections. One consists of World War I armour and equipment, handed down through members of the de Smul family. The other, of uniforms and artefacts of the men who fought in the Salient, belongs to the collector Philippe Oosterlinck. There are some well-interpreted dioramas, clear commentaries and a dramatic stained glass window of the Cloth Hall on fire and outstanding displays of German helmets and décorated shell cases. There is a 1917 German Fokker DR1 and an authentic British 1916 Ford 'T' ambulance, audio-visual presentations, a section dedicated to the finds of 'The Diggers' (qv). British sculptor John Bunting created a statue of Madonna and Child for the museum in memory of **Pte Joseph P. Bunting**, killed 1 July 1916 on the Somme. It stands in a niche above the doorway. A Liverpool Scottish display and other improvements have been added by the enthusiastic Niek and Ilse Benoot-Wateyne who have now taken over the complex. Attached to the Museum is a pleasant modern **Café** with clean WCs. Excellent value appetising sandwich lunch. **Open daily:** 1000-1800. Closed Mondays and January. Tel: + (0) 57 46 84 46. E-mail: info@hoogecrater.com Website:www.hoogecrater.com A small entrance fee is payable with the option of a combined entry fee/lunch.

Walk carefully over the road to the cemetery.

• **Hooge Crater CWGC Cemetery/24.5 miles/10 minutes/Map 1/28**

The cemetery was begun during Third Ypres by the 7th Division's Burial Officer on land that had been heavily fought over in 1915 and 1916 and extended by concentration burials from the surrounding battlefields after the Armistice. There are 5,892 graves registered here, including 2 from the British West Indies and 45 Special Memorials. Over 60% are 'Known Unto God'. The cemetery was designed by Sir Edwin Lutyens assisted by N.A. Rew who also designed the Acheux cemetery on the Somme.

The stone wall that encircles the Stone of Remembrance and which leads to the Cross of Sacrifice at the front of the cemetery is said to be reminiscent of the crater blown across the road on 19 July 1915.

Private Patrick Joseph Bugden, VC, of the 31st Battalion, AIF, who won the medal for his heroic actions at Polygon Wood on 26-27 September 1917, and who was killed on his fifth mission to rescue wounded men under intense fire, is buried here. In the area of the cemetery **2nd Lt Sidney Clayton Woodroffe** of the 8th Bn The Rifle Brigade won his **VC** on 30 July 1915, for gallantly defending his position against the German attack and for leading a counter-attack under intense fire, during which he was killed. His body was lost in subsequent fighting and Woodroffe is commemorated on the Menin Gate. The VC was gazetted on 6 August and on 8 August Woodroffe's friend, the poet Charles Sorley (qv), wrote:

In Memorian S.C.W., VC
There is no fitter end than this.
No need is now to yearn nor sigh.
We know the glory that is his,
A glory that can never die.

Also buried here is **Lt Wilfrid Evelyn Littleboy** of the 16th Bn R Warwicks, killed on 7 October 1917, to whom there is a plaque in Geluveld Church (qv).

Continue down the hill for 500m.

[N.B. Behind the **Canada Café** on the left is the small **Menin Road Museum (Lat & Long: 50.84693 2.93479)** owned by Gregory Florissoone. A typical private collection museum, it has realistic dioramas, some interesting and unusual items including displays of enlistment posters and old private memorial plaques. **Closed** Tues. Tel: + (0)57 20 11 36. E-mail: info@feestzaalcanada.be Small entry fee payable. Visitors' own food may be consumed here provided a drink is bought and the Museum visited.]

Turn left up Canadalaan (Maple Avenue) to the cemetery on the right.

• Sanctuary Wood CWGC Cemetery/25.8 miles/10 minutes/Map 1/28a/50.83838 2.94439

The cemetery contains 102 UK, 41 Canadian and 1 German burial. Here is buried **Lt Gilbert Talbot** of the Rifle Brigade, after whom Talbot House (qv) was named. Son of the Bishop of London and brother of the Rev Neville Talbot, Senior C of E Chaplain of 6th Division, Gilbert was educated at Winchester (where he became friendly with A. P. Herbert) and Christ Church, Oxford, where he was President of the Union and a brilliant debater. In the afternoon of 30 July 1915 he fell, near Zouave Wood, leading a counter-attack with what remained of his men after the brutal liquid fire attack of that morning. Near him as he was shot in the neck cutting the old British barbed wire was his servant, Rifleman Nash, who was shot through the finger as he lay Gilbert's body down. Later attempts by him to return with stretcher bearers to recover Gilbert's body failed, but Nash was later to receive the DCM for his 'devoted care and courage'. Neville Talbot crawled out through the dead of the Rifle Brigade two days later, first finding Woodroffe's body and then Gilbert's. He took his pocket book, prayer book, wrist watch and badge and gave his brother the benediction. A week later he brought the body in and buried it. Killed in the same attack, but whose body although buried and marked, could not be found after the war, was 2nd Lt the Hon G.W. ('Billy') Grenfell, younger brother of Julian Grenfell (qv), the poet. Like Woodroffe, he is commemorated on the Menin Gate. Near to Talbot's grave is that of **Hauptmann Hans Roser, Iron Cross** holder, who was the observer in an Albatross of Field Flying Section 3 which on 25 July 1915 was shot down by a Bristol Scout piloted by Captain Lanoe Hawker. Many British soldiers watched the action, including, it is said, General Plumer. Hawker won the VC for his victories that day. He brought down two other planes in the same action.

The cemetery was designed by Sir Edwin Lutyens with N.A.Rew and its fan-shaped layout is typical of Lutyens' originality.

Outside the cemetery is a **Private Memorial** to **Lt Keith Rae**, also of the Rifle Brigade, killed on the same day. He was last seen at a spot near Hooge Crater in the Château grounds and after the war his family erected this memorial to him on that site. When the last member of the Vink family to own the Château felt that the memorial could no longer be cared for it was moved here and is maintained by the Commonwealth War Graves Commission.

Continue to Sanctuary Wood Museum car park.

• **Sanctuary Wood Museum/Preserved Trenches/25.9 miles/30 minutes/Map 1/29/RWC/Lat & Long: 50.83698 2.94606**
The wood in which the museum is sited is on the forward slopes (Ypres side) of the last ridge before the town. At the top of the road is Hill 62, where a Canadian memorial in the form of a small garden and Stone of Remembrance commemorates the Dominion's efforts in the Salient and in particular the presence in 1914 of the first Canadian troops – Princess Patricia's Light Infantry – to fight against the Germans. During the First Ypres battle the wood still had trees, not yet destroyed by artillery, and it housed a few reserves, medical facilities and dozens of stragglers. Brigadier General Bulfin, of 2nd Division, ordered that the stragglers be left 'in sanctuary' until he instructed what should be done with them – and the wood got its name.

The museum here is owned by Jacques Schier and it is in two parts – the building and the preserved trenches. The building houses the **Café/snackbar** and bookstall, with various military souvenirs on sale, and a Museum. The souvenirs are not exclusively from the First World War, although many of the artefacts on sale were actually found in the Salient. It is always sensible to be cautious about remnants of bullets and shells and collectors should never pick up anything on the battlefield itself. At the heart of the collection are the dozen or so 3-D wooden viewing cabinets. They are a must. Each one has different glass slides that when viewed with persistence focus dramatically into sharp 3 dimensions. Here in this atmospheric environment is the true horror of war – dead horses, bodies in trees, heads and legs in trenches and, everywhere, mud, mud, mud. The history of the pictures is obscure. Jacques maintains that they are Belgian, others say that they were once owned by the Imperial War Museum and disposed of during a clean-out in the 1950s. At the back of the museum, past hardware so rusty that is difficult to see how it keeps heart and soul together, are the trenches. They are original in the way that George Washington's axe, with three new heads and two new handles, is original. Yet they follow the shape and nature of the original trenches, which were

Preserved trenches, Sanctuary Wood.

designed to twist and turn so that invaders were always isolated in a short length of trench and could not set up machine guns to mow down the defenders in lines. They smell, but not with the stench of death that hung over the Salient for four long years. They are damp, probably with water underfoot, and in the middle is a concrete tunnel, passable to the wellie brigade. It defies the imagination to conjure up a picture of trenches in belts up to a mile or more wide joined in chicken-wire patterns and stretching from the North Sea to Switzerland – but that was how it was.

Open all year round during daylight hours. An entrance fee is payable. Tel: + (0) 57 46 63 73.

Some 300 yards further up the road is the **Canadian Memorial at Hill 62 ('Mount Sorrel')**, Lat & Long: 50.83515 2.94721.

Return to the Menin Road, turn left and drive to the first roundabout. By the third exit is

• Hellfire Corner Demarcation Stone/27.5 miles/5 minutes/Map 1/30/Lat & Long: 50.84893 2.91586

This is Hellfire Corner. It was under constant observation by Germans on the high ground and anything that moved across it was shelled. Canvas screens were erected beside the road in an attempt to conceal movement.

By the roadside as you drive round the roundabout is a **Demarcation Stone** (one of twelve surviving in the Salient) to mark the Germans' nearest point to Ypres. It now bears an explanatory plaque. The metre-high stones, made from pink Alsace granite were designed by the sculptor Paul Moreau-Vauthier who had been seriously wounded while serving as a machine gunner at Verdun and who first conceived the stone at the Salon des Artistes Décorateurs in 1919. It was made by the stonemason Léon Telle and had three patterns: the Belgian, surmounted by a 'Jass's' casque, with, on its sides, a typical Belgian water bottle and gas mask; the British, surmounted by a Tommy's tin helmet, with a British water bottle and small box respirator, and the French, surmounted by a *Poilu*'s casque, with on its sides a typical French water (or wine!) bottle and gas mask. Beneath the helmet was a laurel wreath. All bore inscriptions in the three languages: 'Here the invader was brought to a standstill 1918'; *'Hier werd de overweldiger tot staan gebrackt 1918'* and *'Ici fut arrêté l'envahisseur 1918'* (preferred to a proposed *'Ici fut brisé l'élan des Barbares'*! 'Here the thrust of the barbarian was broken') and the name of the appropriate sector. At each corner was a palm emerging from a hand grenade.

They were erected by the Touring Club of France, supported by the Belgian Touring Club and the Ypres League and erected in the early 1920s, their sites having been decided by Marshal Pétain and his staff. They were to mark the length of the Front Line from the North Sea to the Vosges. Accounts vary wildly as to how many actually were erected – from 119 (Rose Coombs) to 280 (Swinton's Twenty Years After). There were probably 118 'official' stones. The history of the stones is being researched by Rik Scherpenberg whose web site details his findings (www.geocities.com/demarcationstones/).

Take the last (Zillebeke) exit from the roundabout.

Perth China Wall CWGC Cemetery (Lat & Long: 50.84200 2.92080) is passed on the left.

Continue through the village of Zillebeke, turning left at the T junction after the church following signs to Maple Copse CWGC Cemetery, but before reaching it turn right following signs (easily missed) to Hill 60 just before the woods. Stop at the café on the right.

• Hill 60/Memorials/29.7 miles/20 minutes/RWC/Map 1/31, 1/32/Lat & Long: 50.82468 2.92975

Here is a Memorial to **Queen Victoria's Rifles**, plus small craters, a blockhouse and across the road the smart **Hill 60 Tearoom/Restaurant**, Tel: + (0)57 20 88 60. It replaces the museum run for many years by a member of the Schier (cf) family, thus ending a long tradition at Hill 60. It was originally maintained by the Queen Victoria's Rifles. The 'Hill' was formed by the spoil taken from the cutting through which the railway runs (200 yards further up the road) and gets its name because the resultant feature is 60 metres above sea level and forms an extension to the Messines Ridge. The French lost the Hill to the Germans in 1914 and when the British took over from them following the race to the sea it was then decided that the feature must be retaken. Much of the fighting here was underground and it was probably here that the first British mine of the war was blown by Lt White, RE on 17 February 1915 – though the tunnelling had actually been taken over from the French. Later it was decided that a major mining operation should be undertaken and the job was given to 173rd Tunnelling Company, RE. Work began early in March 1915 and three tunnels were begun towards the German line about 50 yards away, a pit having first been dug some 16 ft deep. Almost immediately the miners came upon dead bodies and quick-lime was brought up to cover them and the bodies were dragged out. It was hot, unpleasant and dangerous work. Apart from the constant threat that the tunnel would collapse and bury the miners alive, there was the possibility of poison gas and not least that the enemy might break into the tunnel or explode a mine of his own below it. By the time that the digging was finished the tunnels stretched more than 100 yards, and dragging the ninety-four 100 lb bags of gunpowder to the mineheads, winching them down the shafts and then manoeuvring them along the tunnels was a Herculean task. On 15 April all the charges were ready and on 17 April at 1905 hours the mine was fired. The explosion built up over 10 seconds throwing volcano-like debris nearly 300 ft high and for 300 yards all around. Simultaneously British, French and Belgian guns opened an artillery barrage and encouraged by regimental buglers the Royal West Kents fixed bayonets and charged the dazed Germans of the 172nd Infantry Regiment, killing about 150 for only seven casualties of their own. The Hill was won. Three days later **Lt Geoffrey Harold Woolley** won the **first Territorial Army VC** in resisting a German counter-attack. His citation reads, 'For most conspicuous bravery on Hill 60 during the night of 20-21 April 1915. Although the only officer on the hill at the time, and with very few men, he successfully resisted all attacks on his trench and continued throwing bombs and encouraging his men till relieved. His trench during all the time was being heavily shelled and bombed, and was subjected to heavy machine-gun fire by the enemy.' Woolley was a member of the 9th

London Regiment, Queen Victoria's Rifles who had, with the Royal West Kents and King's Own Scottish Borderers, taken part in the initial assault on 17 April. Underground warfare went on here for another 10 months until the beginning of Third Ypres. Many of the men who worked and fought in those black corridors in the clay died there and are there still. Hill 60 is a cemetery.

Beyond the enclosed area on the left are **Memorials to the 14th (Light) Division and the 1st Australian Tunnelling Company** with Information Panels. **OP.** Standing with one's back to the Memorials the spires of Ypres can be seen straight ahead. **(Lat & Long: 50.82410 2.9806).**

The hitherto inaccessible **Caterpillar Crater**, to the left, past the WW2 Memorial, can now be visited with care along a small footpath.

Continue over the railway and turn right towards Ypres at the T junction.
Continue to the first left turn (Vaartstraat) with a signboard to several CWGC Cemeteries.
Turn left and continue. Kemmel Hill can be seen straight ahead.

CWGC Cemeteries **Chester Farm (Lat & Long: 50. 82106 2.90156)** and **Spoilbank (Lat & Long: 50.81998 2.89966)** are passed on the right.

Continue to the T junction and turn left. Continue to the roundabout. Take the N336 signed Armentières and immediately stop on the right.

• Monument to St Eloi Tunnellers/Craters/32.3 miles/15 minutes/ Map 1/33, 1/34/Lat & Long: 50.81002 2.89206

This memorial was erected on 11 November 2001 to 172nd Tunnelling Coy 3rd Br Div, 2nd Can Div and 7th Belg Fld Arty. T. E. Hulme (qv) served in the trenches at St Eloi in the spring of 1915 and wrote a poem Trenches: St Eloi, which expresses the mind-numbing emptiness and apparent futility of trench warfare:

... Behind the line, cannon, hidden, lying back miles.

Before the line, chaos:

My mind is a corridor. The minds about me are corridors.

Nothing suggests itself. There is nothing to do but keep on.

Hulme was wounded in the arm here on 14 April 1915, with a 'Blighty one'. An extract from his poem is inscribed on the memorial. The British flag flies beside it and in 2003 a Krupp gun was added.

Two of the **craters blown here on 27 March 1916 and 7 June 1917** are now visitable one on each side of the road. On the right after some 50 yards is an Information Board about the 7 June 1917 mine and a wooden path through a locked gate leads to the impressive water-filled crater where there is a seat and more Information Boards. A trail round the crater leads to a well-preserved bunker. **N.B.** To enter you must ring the Tourist Office in Ieper (+ (0) 57 23 92 20) giving your name and mobile phone no. You will then be given a key code

Queen Victoria's Rifles Memorial, Hill 60.

Memorial to 14th (Light)
Division, Hill 60.

to enter the complex. Well worth the effort. The crater to the left is up the small path to the left behind the telephone tower (by the 'Golf' sign) and easily accessible though on private land. It was created by one of six mines blown astride the old German front line at 0415 hours on 27 March 1916. Shafts dug to position the mines were up to 55ft deep and took more than 8 months to prepare. The mines were blown as part of an assault by 9th Brigade, after which most of the 4th Royal Fusiliers' objectives were still in enemy hands. Casualties were forty officers and 809 other ranks. On 3 April, 76th Brigade was brought in to reinforce a new attack. During the assault the Brigade Major, Capt Billy Congreve (qv), reached the rim of one of the craters. He wrote in his diary:

'Imagine my surprise and horror when I saw a whole crowd of armed Boches! I stood there for a moment feeling a bit sort of shy, and then I levelled my revolver at the nearest Boche and shouted, 'Hands up, all the lot of you!' A few went up at once, then a few more and then the lot; and I felt the proudest fellow in the world as I cursed them.'

Congreve brought in four officers and sixty-eight men – though other accounts make it five officers and seventy-seven men – for which he was recommended for the **VC** (which he was not to receive until July 1916 and then posthumously after further acts of bravery on the Somme) and awarded the DSO. He is buried in Corbie Communal Cemetery on the Somme.

Today the water-filled crater is stocked with fish.

Turn round and at the roundabout take the N365 signed to Mesen and continue to Wijtschate.

• Wijtschate

Nicknamed 'Whitesheet' by the Tommies, fighting began around here in the first year of the war. The Germans held this area of high ground despite efforts by both the British and the French to take it. In the first, Messines, phase of the Third Battle of Ypres, the village was taken by the 36th (Ulster) Division and the 16th (South of Ireland) Division. On 3 July 1917 General Plumer presented King Albert of the Belgians with the church bell which had been dug out of the ruins. Serving near Wijtschate from 6 June 1917 with 224th Siege Battery RGA was the vorticist artist, writer and philosopher, **Wyndham Lewis**. On 14 June he wrote to Ezra Pound, 'Imagine a stretch of land one mile in depth sloping up from the old German first-line to the top of a ridge, stretching to right and left as far as you can see. It looks very large, never-ending and empty. There are only occasional little groups of men around a bomb-dump, or building a light railway: two men pushing a small truck on which a man is being brought back lying on his stomach, his head hanging over the side. The edge of the ridge is where you are bound for, at the corner of a demolished wood. The place is either loathesomely hot, or chilly according to the time of day at which you cross it. It is a reddish colour, and all pits, ditches & chasms, & black stakes, several hundred, here & there, marking the map-position of a wood.' Later in June Lewis contracted trench fever and was hospitalised in Boulogne.

Memorial to the Tunnellers, & Krupp Kanon, St Eloi.

On entering Wijtschate take the right turn signed Kemmel. Continue into the main square and keeping to the right of the bandstand turn right direction Dikkebus/Sporthaal.

• Statue of 'The Miner'/33.8 miles/5 minutes

Unveiled on 31 October 2008, the fine statue is by Jan Dieusaert. Beside it are Information Boards about the Battles for Wijtschate and Bayernwald and Tunnelling.

Continue to the right turn signed to Croonaert Chapel Cemetery. Continue to the path (which is 200m long) to the left to the cemetery.

• Memorial to 1st Chasseurs à Pied/Croonaert Chapel CWGC Cemetery/35.3 miles/15 minutes/Map 1/42, 1/41/Lat & Long: 50.80150 2.87510

At this point there is a grey **stone Memorial to Lt Lasmer, 11 'Sous Officiers' and 174 Corporals and Chasseurs of the 1st Bn Chasseurs à Pied** who fell here in the defence of Belgium and France in the fighting of 3-15 November 1914. It was unveiled on 9 June 1935 when 90 veterans of the regiment came from all corners of France to pay homage to their old comrades with their old commanding officer, General Somon. By standing with your back to the memorial the spires of Ypres are seen straight ahead while immediately behind is Kemmel Hill. In **Croonaert Chapel Cemetery** there are 75 burials, seven of which are unknown. After the Armistice 51 German graves from 1917 were removed. The grave of **Chang Chi Hsuen** of the Chinese Labour Corps, 23 January 1919 lies in a separate plot just within the entrance. The cemetery, which was designed by W.C Von Berg who had served with the London Rifles during the war, was begun in June 1917 by 19th Division and used until the following November. Two later burials were made in April 1918 and January 1919.

Turn round and return towards Wijtschate. Park on the right just after the turning to the left.

In the field to the right was the site of the original Croonaert Chapel painted by Adolf Hitler who fought in this area in the 16th BRIR.

Walk back to the junction, turn right by a Diorama Board looking towards Ieper and continue to the entrance to Bayernwald on the right.

It is entered by a gate controlled by a coded lock. **N.B.** To enter you will first have had to pay the small entrance fee and obtained the code from the Tourist Office at Kemmel (qv). This is in the green 'De Bergen' Centre at the crossroads as one enters Kemmel. Tel: + (0) 57 45 04 55. E-mail: toerisme@heuvelland.be **Open:** weekdays 0900-1200 and 1315-1700. Sat/Sun: 1000-1200 and from 1 April-30 October also from 1400-1700. As the trenches are on private land there will be no access on occasional hunting days!

• Bayernwald Trenchlines and Mine Shaft/35.4 miles/15 minutes/ Map 1/43/Lat & Long: 50.80137 2.87672

Standing with one's back to the entrance one is overlooking the British lines under which they tunnelled to lay mines in preparation for the Messines assault of 1917. The Germans saw evidence of this work and within the area of the wood constructed sophisticated underground listening posts with special equipment to track the progress of the British tunnels with the aim of intercepting them with even deeper mines.

This area was known to the Germans as Bayernwald, a name decreed by Prince Rupprecht as a tribute to the Bavarian troops who served here. Also known as Bois Quarante (its height in metres i.e. 40) the site was owned for many years by M. Becquaert (Senior) who operated an idiosyncratic museum here. After his death the site was left to deteriorate but it has now been sold and the present owner granted permission (a 26-year concession) to the ABAF (qv) to excavate the interesting network of trenches, dugouts and the deep mineshafts. Together with the Commune of Heuvelland they have restored 4 exceptional concrete bunkers, two deep German counter-mine shafts constructed to listen for British workings and about 100m of the trench system from the main German 1916-17 line. The 320 m of trenches have been made using A frames that stand clear of the original floor and show the typical German construction of wattle wall re-inforcement and planking, rather than duck boards. Unfortunately, as in 1917, the trenches are susceptible to flooding and may not always be accessible. There is a wooden shelter with Information Boards and a splendid bronze *bas relief* map of the Salient from the Bluff to Messines, showing all the mines - exploded and non-exploded - and the 17 visible craters. Six moderate sized 'Bertha' mines were laid here. This is a fascinating battlefield reconstruction site and well merits a visit. The site will be renovated for the 100th Anniversaries starting in 2014.

Continue and turn first right along Hollandseschuur (ignoring the restriction sign) to the T junction.

[**N.B.** By turning right here and continuing some 250m to the right the **Hollandseschuur Craters** are found near the farm buildings to the right on private land (**Map 1/40**). The aim of this mine was to take out a small enemy salient into our lines. Three charges were fired in November 1917 at the end of a 250metre tunnel dug by 250th Tunnelling Coy.]

Turn left onto Vierstraat. Continue to the farm on the right and pull in at the end of the farm buildings.

Ahead in the meadow to the right is a distinct dip running alonside the road leading up to 5 tall poplar-like trees. This is the site of the **Sunken Road painted by Adolf Hitler in 1914 (Lat & Long: 50.79427 2.87240)**.

Continue to Wijtschate Square. Turn right following signs to Kemmel and continue to the cemetery on the right.

Bayernwald reconstructed trenches showing plank and wattles.

The path to Spanbroekmolen (Pool of Peace).

The Peckham Farm Crater.

• *Wytschaete Military CWGC Cemetery/16th Irish & 36th (Ulster) Div Memorials/37.0 miles/5 minutes/ Map 1/44, 1/45/Lat & Long: 50.78452 2.87673*

Containing 486 UK, 31 Australian, 19 Canadian, 7 New Zealand, 11 South African, 1 German, 25 special memorials and 673 unknown burials, the cemetery was created after the Armistice by concentration of graves from the surrounding battlefields. Here are the graves of **Drummer James Etak McKay**, 1st/4th Gordon Highlanders, 19 March 1915 age 20 and **2nd Lt John Victor Ariel**, 45th Sqn RFC, age 20 who 'Died of wounds received in aerial combat 7 July 1916'. The cemetery was designed by Sir Edwin Lutyens with W.H. Cowlishaw. Just beyond it is the **Memorial to the 16th Irish Div** who captured Wijtschate on 7 June 1917. On 10 June 2007 as part of the 90th Anniversary Commemorations, two new **Memorials** were inaugurated some 800m further down this road, to the **36th (Ulster) Div** on the left and the **16th (Irish) Division** on the right **(Lat & Long: 50.78196 2.86568),** on the spot where they fought literally side by side for the first time.

Continue to a green CWGC sign to the left to Spanbroekmolen Cemetery.

A short distance up the road to the left (and only visible from that road) is the large water-filled **Peckham Farm Crater (Lat & Long: 50.77967 2.86301)**.

Continue along Wijschatestraat (which was known as Suicide Road) to the CWGC sign to Lone Tree Cemetery to the left and turn left along Kruisstraat. Stop on the left at the entrance to the Spanbroekmolen crater.

• *Spanbroekmolen (Pool of Peace)/38.3 miles/10 minutes/Map 1/46/Lat & Long: 50.77558 2.86124*

Named for the windmill that stood here for three centuries until it was destroyed by the Germans on 1 November 1914, this is the site of what was probably the largest mine explosion of the nineteen blown on 7 June 1917, at the start of the Messines phase of the Third Battle of Ypres. It consisted of 91,000lbs of ammonal.

Following a seven-day bombardment the battle opened with nine divisions of infantry advancing on a 9-mile front. They came towards you from the west. They had been told to advance at zero hour, 0310, whether the mines had blown or not. Spanbroekmolen went up 15 seconds late, killing a number of our own soldiers from the 36th Ulster Division, some of whom are buried in the cemetery ahead. The war diary of the 3rd Bn Worcester Regiment, that attacked a little south of here, records for that day, 'Battalion casualties were heavy and difficult to account for – a fair proportion must have been caused by our own barrage'.

Sir Philip Gibbs (qv), the war correspondent, described the scene thus,

'Suddenly at dawn, as a signal for all of our guns to open fire, there rose out of the dark ridge of Messines and "Whitesheet" and that ill-famed Hill 60, enormous volumes of scarlet flame from nineteen separate mines, throwing up high towers of earth and smoke all lighted by the flame, spilling over into fountains of fierce colour, so that many of our soldiers waiting for the assault were thrown to the ground. The German troops were stunned, dazed and horror-stricken if they were not killed outright. Many of them lay dead in the great craters opened by the mines.'

On 12 March 1915 an attack on the mill (coming from the direction of Kemmel) then in German hands, was used by the British as a diversionary action during the Neuve Chapelle battle as a means of drawing away enemy reserves. The 1st Wiltshires and 3rd Worcesters achieved little and incurred heavy losses.

In September 1929 Tubby Clayton wrote to *The Times* to point out that the last of the big craters at St Eloi, now 'a pool of rare perfection', was in danger of being lost in plans to extend the village. Two major craters, however, still remain visible in the village today (see page 74). Tubby's letter prompted discussions which led to Lord Wakefield buying the Spanbroekmolen Crater. It was renamed 'The Pool of Peace' and then left untouched as a memorial. On 22 April 1985 (the seventieth anniversary of the inauguration of Talbot House) Princess Alexandra visited the Pool and planted two mountain ash trees. She was due to be accompanied by her husband, the Hon Angus Ogilvy, who was Patron of Toc H, but he was ill and could not travel. Nevertheless he was mentioned on the commemorative plaque that was erected at the time at the entrance. However on 2 June 1992 the site was listed as an area 'of outstanding natural beauty' and therefore subject to the attendant rules and regulations. This included the removal of this plaque. (It is planned in the future to erect one plaque which will tell the history of the Pool of Peace.) After the listing a new wooden gate and fence were erected and the perimeter cleared. Visitors can walk all the way round the original borders.

Continue a few yards to just beyond the path on the right to the cemetery.

From this point a superb view over the Messines battlefield can be had. Looking back down the road the bulk of Kemmel Hill is clearly visible and looking forward along the road Messines Church can be seen on the Ridge. To the left on the skyline is Wijtschate Church and to the right the Irish Peace Tower.

• Lone Tree CWGC Cemetery/38.3 miles/10 minutes/Map 1/47

The cemetery contains 88 UK burials and 6 unknown, many of them of the RI Rifles (36th) Division, killed on 7 June 1917, some by our own mine.

Continue, to the next crossroads and turn right along Wulvergemstraat (once known as Pill Road). On the crest of the hill, before the house on the right are some large craters. Stop.

• Kruisstraat Craters/38.9 miles/10 minutes/Map 1/48/Lat & Long: 50.77014 2.86491

You are now standing on the German front line at the beginning (7 June 1917) Messines Phase, of Third Ypres. The attack came from the direction of Kemmel Hill (which can be seen just beyond the craters) passed over the area where you now are, down into the valley and up onto the Messines Ridge where the distinctive shape of Messines Church can be seen.

These two craters are legacies of the mines blown at the start of Third Ypres. The digging was begun by 250th Tunnelling Coy in December 1915, handed over to 182nd Company at the beginning of January 1916, and to 3rd Canadian at the end of the month. In April, 175th Tunnelling Coy briefly took charge and when the gallery reached 1,051ft it was handed over to 171st Coy who were also responsible for Spanbroekmolen.

At 1,605ft a charge of 30,000lb of ammonal was laid and at the end of a small branch of 166ft to the right a second charge of 30,000lb was placed under the German front line. This completed the original plan, but it was decided to extend the mining to a position under the German third line. Despite meeting clay and being inundated with water underground which necessitated the digging of a sump, in just two months a gallery stretching almost half a mile from the shaft was completed and a further charge of 30,000lb of ammonal placed. This tunnel was the longest of any of the Third Ypres mines. In February 1917 enemy counter-measures necessitated some repair to one of the chambers and the opportunity was taken to place a further charge of 19,500lb making a total of four mines all of which were ready by 9 May 1917.

The two craters that remain, probably the first two charges, are favourite fishing spots for licence holders.

Return to the crossroads and turn right towards Mesen (Messines). At the next T junction turn left and stop immediately on the right.

• Messines Ridge British CWGC Cemetery/New Zealand Memorial/40.3 miles/10 minutes/ Map 1/49, 1/50/Lat Long: 50.76532 2.89085

Created after the Armistice, the cemetery contains 986 UK, 332 Australian, 1 Canadian, 115 New Zealand, 56 South African, 954 unknown and a large number of special memorials. At the entrance to the cemetery is the **New Zealand Memorial**, listing 840 men killed in the Salient and who have no known

Messines Ridge British Cemetery and New Zealand Memorial.

The distinctive outline of Messines Church.

graves, following their policy not to list their missing on the Menin Gate. The New Zealand Memorials are all in cemeteries chosen as appropriate to the fighting in which the men died. This cemetery and memorial were designed by Charles Holden (who also designed the New Zealand Memorial at Polygon Wood).

On 7 June 1917, during the Messines action which was the prelude to Third Ypres, one of the war's most beloved Padres was awarded the Military Cross for his work on the Messines Ridge. The citation which was published in the *London Gazette* of 16 August reads,

'For conspicuous gallantry and devotion to duty. He showed the greatest courage and disregard of his own safety in attending wounded under heavy fire. He searched shell holes for our own and enemy wounded, assisting them to the dressing station, and his cheerfulness and endurance had a splendid effect upon all ranks, whom he constantly visited.'

Interior of Messines Museum.

New Zealand Memorial and Bunker, Messines Ridge Memorial Park.

This brave Padre was the **Rev Geoffrey Anketell Studdert Kennedy, Chaplain to the Forces**, then serving with 17th Bde of 24th Division and better known as 'Woodbine Willie'. This unconventional Padre endeared himself to the men for his habit of doling out Woodbine cigarettes, for using their own strong language when he felt it necessary, and because he questioned his own faith when confronted by the cruel carnage around him. His *Rough Rhymes of a Padre* expressed his love for his fellow soldiers and his understanding of their love of each other, as exemplified in the poem, *His Mate*, which describes the burial of a soldier and whose last verse is,

There are many kinds of sorrow
In this world of Love and Hate,
But there is no sterner sorrow
Than a soldier's for his mate.

Buried here is **Usko Leonard Salonen** 'of Finland' serving with the 39th AIF, killed 8 June 1917 aged 29. Born in Finland in 1887 he had emigrated to Australia at the age of 18 and enlisted in 1916 at the same time as his uncle Axel Alexander Olin who was killed in 1918 and is buried in the Berks Cemetery Extension Plugstreet.

From the top of the cemetery the Island of Ireland Tower can be seen.

Continue along Nieuwkerkestraat to the crossroads with the N365.

Extra Visit to the London Scottish Memorial (Map 1/51) Round trip: 1.5 miles. Approximate time: 10 minutes/Lat & Long: 50.77256 2.89303
Turn left and continue to the memorial on the right.
The inscription on the grey granite Celtic Cross records how near this spot on Halloween 1914 the London Scottish came into action, being the first territorial Battalion to engage the enemy. The battalion lost 394 of their 700 strength in the action. It was erected to the memory of all the Officers, NCOs and men of the Regiment who fell in the Great War, 1914-1919 and shows its Battle Honours year by year.
Turn round and return to Nieuwkerkestraat and pick up the main itinerary.

Turn right at the crossroads along the N365 into Mesen and first left following signs to Bethleem Farm CWGC Cemetery. Park near the bandstand.

• Messines (Mesen)/Museum/RB/Memorials/40.7 miles/10 minutes/Map 1/35, 1/36/Lat & Long: 50.76541 2.89808
On the left, in the Town Hall of this 'the smallest city in Belgium', is a small **Museum** only open on application (Tel: + (0) 57 44 405 11). It contains

weaponry, artefacts, photos and documents relating to the war. To the right is a small group of memorials including a New Zealand Kowhai tree, planted on 11 November 1993 (the 75th Anniversary of the Armistice). The New Zealand Ambassador comes to Messines each year to celebrate ANZAC Day and Messines is associated with the New Zealand town of Featherston, where some 8,000 NZ soldiers trained before coming to the Western Front. There is also a Ross Bastiaan Australian bronze relief memorial tablet and a Japanese International Peace Post (qv) unveiled on 17 September 1989 by the artist, Miss Mié Tabé, and given to Messines by the Japanese Peace Movement. Its message says 'May Peace Rule the World'.

Turn right before the bandstand to the Church. This was the subject of a painting by Cpl Adolf Hitler when he was posted in the area with the 16th Bavarian Reserve Infantry from November 1914 to March 1915 and purportedly treated in the crypt which served as a German Field Hospital when he was wounded in the arm. It now contains an extraordinary carillon whose bells were contributed by many Belgian and Allied organisations.

Continue back to the main road and continue on the N365 direction Ploegsteert. After some 400m turn right following signs to the New Zealand Memorial. Park at the entrance.

• New Zealand Memorial and Park/Bunkers/41.2 miles/15 minutes/Map 1/52/OP/Lat & Long: 50.76076 2.89098

This memorial is identical to that at s-Graventafel (qv). It was unveiled on 1 August 1924 by King Albert I of the Belgians and overlooks a memorial park at the foot of which are two large, well-preserved German pill boxes.

It was well known that the Germans were constructing numbers of pill boxes on the Messines Ridge and prior to the opening of Third Ypres frequent patrols were made into German lines in order to find out more about the defences. The New Zealanders maintained daily intelligence summaries on the current state of the defences and their engineers blew up concrete dugouts half a mile south of here at Petite Douve Farm (qv) barely two days before the offensive opened. These two pill boxes appear identical, but the one on the left was made in situ while the other was put together with concrete blocks, probably to a pre-fabricated design.

On 7 June the attack here was led by the 3rd New Zealand Rifle Brigade advancing broadly from the direction of Nieuwkerke and the bunkers were taken in the first hour.

From the stand between the bunkers a good view of the Messines battlefield can be had provided trees do not obscure the view. The front lines here were about 700 yards away. Take straight ahead as 12 o'clock. At 1 o'clock the church on the skyline is Nieuwkerke. At 11 o'clock on the horizon are the spires of Armentières.

Standing outside the park, with one's back to the entrance, look straight towards the hills ahead and take that as 12 o'clock. At 10 o'clock in the middle distance is the spire of Wulvergem Church roughly 1,500 yards away. Moving towards 12 o'clock is the tall wireless mast of Mont des Cats, then Mont Noir and next to it, the tallest hill, Kemmel, with a smaller radio mast. At 12 o'clock on the horizon are the bushes which surround Spanbroekmolen.

Return to the N365 and follow signs to Ploegsteert and Armentières. Continue downhill to the tower on the right.

• Island of Ireland Peace Park and Tower/41.7 miles/15 minutes/ Map 1/37/Lat & Long: 50.75979 2.89572

For many years following the Armistice, during the turbulent period leading to the formation of the Irish Free State, men from Southern Ireland who fought with

The Island of Ireland Peace Tower.

the British in the Great War were often considered as 'traitors' and their sacrifice deliberately forgotten. In an overdue gesture of remembrance and reconciliation between nationalists and unionists this imposing grey stone tower is dedicated to the memory of all those from the Island of Ireland who fought and died in the First World War. The Tower was the brainchild of Catholic Nationalist MP Paddy Harte and Protestant Unionist Glen Barr who visited the area together in 1996 and conceived the project as 'A Journey of Reconciliation'.

It was unveiled on 11 November 1998 by President Mary McAlease and Queen Elizabeth II in the presence of the King and Queen of the Belgians. This site was chosen as it stands on the Messines

Ridge where men from the north and the south of the Island fought almost shoulder to shoulder in June 1917.

As one passes through the entrance in the grey stone walls there are polished granite Information Plaques in Belgian, French, English and Gaelic leading up to the tower itself. They include some moving quotations from the poets Francis Ledwidge (qv) and Tom Kettle, from the Official War Artist, Sir William Orpen,

Chaplain Francis Gleeson of the R Munster Fusiliers and others who served with Irish Regiments. Other plaques salute the memory of the 10th (Irish) Division which lost 9,363 men, the 16th (Irish) Division which lost 28,398 and the 36th (Ulster) Division which lost 32,186. In the room at the base of the slim Tower, a traditional Irish form which has been built in Ireland since the 8th Century, are beautiful bronze boxes made to contain the names of the Irish casualties and a Visitor's Book.

The park surrounding the tower includes four gardens for the four Provinces with four different types of tree representing the Irish soldiers marching towards the tower. Owing to financial difficulties experienced by the originators, the park is now maintained by the Commonwealth War Graves Commission.

Continue downhill. Just before the bottom of the hill on the right hand side is La Petite Douve Farm. Under this farm many experts believe is one of the powerful remaining unexploded mines set to fire on 7 June 1917.

Continue to a left turn to the group of CWGC signs to Mud Corner, Prowse Point etc.

On the slope to the right is the site of the old Château de la Hutte on Hill 63 under which the British built large subterranean shelters. At one time it was planned to build the Ploegsteert Memorial here.

> **Extra Visit to Prowse Point CWGC Cemetery (Map 1/53, Lat & Long: 50.74431 2.89887), St Yvon Christmas Truce Cross (Map 1/54, Lat & Long: 50.74438 2.90257) and Bairnsfather Plaque (Map 1/55, Lat & Long: 50.74298 2.90404) Round trip: 1.4 miles. Approximate time: 30 minutes.**
>
> *Turn left and continue along the Chemin du Mont de la Hutte to the cemetery on the right.*
>
> **Prowse Point Military CWGC Cemetery**
>
> Designed by W.K.Cowlishaw, this lovely cemetery with an unusual irregular layout was named after Brig-Gen C.B. ('Bertie') Prowse, DSO, who fell on 1 July 1916, and is buried at Louvencourt on the Somme. It was begun by the Dublin Fusiliers and the 1st Warwicks and was used

Extra Visit continued

from as early as November 1914 until April 1918 and contains 159 UK, 42 New Zealand, 13 Australian, 1 Canadian and 12 German prisoner burials. At the front of the cemetery is a rectangular pond with water lillies. The roof of a small bunker that existed during the war can still be seen in the lawn to the right of the graves area.

Also buried in Louvencourt CWGC Cemetery is the poet, Lt Roland Aubrey Leighton, probably best known for being the fiancé of Vera Brittain, author of Testament of Youth. On 12 April 1915, Leighton's battalion, the 7th Worcesters, reached trenches in Plugstreet Wood. Here he wrote the poem to Vera entitled Villanelle,

> Violets from Plug Street Wood,
> Sweet, I send you oversea.

(Violets from Oversea, the first line of the last verse, gave us the title of the first edition of our book on twenty-five poets of World War I). Leighton was killed on 23 December 1916.

Another poet was Charles Sorley (qv) of the 7th Suffolk Regt serving to the south of Ploegsteert Wood in July 1915. In his letters Sorley describes a bombing raid on a 'redoubt of some kind' the Germans were making and upon which the battalion did not have enough shells to fire. Although some bombs (grenades) were thrown, the Germans soon raked the ground 'with an absolute hail of rifle and machine-gun fire'. Many of the raiding Suffolks were wounded. Nevertheless the officer leading the raid, described only as 'C' by Sorley, was noticed the next day on trench patrol, 'dressed in summer get-up; gum boot, breeches, shirt-sleeves, sambrown belt and pistol. He had a bandage round his head, but only a very slight scratch from a fragment of bomb. He was walking along, reading from his German pocket edition of Faust.'

Several recent burials of remains found in the vicinity have been made here, notably that of Pte A.J. Mather, 33rd Bn AIF, died 8 June 1917 age 37. His body having been found in Ploegsteeert Wood and identified through painstaking DNA matching with a 97 year old cousin, Pte Mather was reinterred here with full military honours In the presence of 7 family members and Lt Gen Ken Gillespie, Chief of the Australian Army, on 22 July 2010.

To the right just beyond the cemetery is a path which leads to **Mud Corner**, **Toronto Avenue**, **Ploegsteert Wood Mil** and **Rifle House** CWGC Cemeteries. It would take about an hour to walk to all of them and back to the road. They are in what was the infamous 'Plugstreet' Wood. The Wood is about 2,000 yards wide, east to west, and about 1,000 yds, north to south. Critical fighting for possession of it took place in 1914, between mid-October and the beginning of November – known as the Battle of Armentières. It ran, therefore, concurrently with First Ypres and Ploegsteert and marks the bottom end of the Salient. A fine bayonet charge by the 1st Somersets (their '1st in France', as the Regimental History puts it – although they were in fact in Belgium) stopped one German attack on the village of le Gheer at the south-east corner of the wood. Conditions in the wood were abominable. The Somerset History records,

'On 25 October ... the trenches were absolute quagmires ... the water and mud were ankle deep in the front lines; by the beginning of November the trenches were knee-deep in slime and filth. The stench from dead bodies often partially buried in the soggy, slimy ground, just as they had fallen, was awful. Unwashed, caked with mud, clothes sodden... aching with rheumatism and the early symptoms of trench feet, verminous and generally in a deplorable condition [the Somersets] held the line with a degree of staunchness, determination and cheerfulness of spirit never surpassed in the whole glorious history of the Army.'

Although they made excursions into the eastern edge, the Germans never took the wood.

Continue to the cross in the bank on the left.

Khaki Chums' Christmas Truce Cross

A simple wooden cross was erected here by the Khaki Chums Association for Military Remembrance when they spent a cold Christmas in the area to commemorate the 85th Anniversary of the Truce. On 13 December 2003 a more substantial Cross was dedicated. In 2010 it was decorated with footballs and a small Christmas Tree.

You are now in the village of St Yvon. Here the cartoonist **Capt Bruce Bairnsfather** (qv), then a Lieutenant, was billetted and created his immortal character, 'Old Bill'. Bairnsfather, a trained artist who had previously served in the Royal Warwickshires before the war, rejoined the colours in August 1914 and by November was with the 1st Battalion here in the trenches at Plugstreet Wood. Possessed with sharp powers of observation and a quick pencil he began to draw cartoons to amuse his men – on anything that was to hand, from ammunition boxes to walls. Just behind the regiment's lines in this village he and a fellow officer called Hudson took over the ruins of a cottage with a more or less intact cellar,

Khaki Chums Christmas Truce Cross, St Yvon.

Plaque on the cottage on the site of the dugout where Bairnsfather drew his first cartoon.

The beautiful cemetery at Prowse Point with headstone of newly re-interred Pte A.J. Mather, 22 July 2010.

Extra Visit continued

which they converted into a dugout for living quarters. On the dugout's walls Bairnsfather amused himself by sketching the situations that he was experiencing in the area.

Continue, past a pond at the bend to the right, to the first house on the right.

Commemorative Plaque to Capt Bruce Bairnsfather on House No. 12 Chemin du Mont de la Hutte.

This house has been built on the very site of that billet. On one occasion when several of them were in the cottage, the Germans began to shell the village and, knowing that the enemy would have ranged his guns on the buildings, they dashed outside and took cover in a nearby ditch. At last when the shelling seemed to be over they went back into the cottage and just as they did so a heavy shell landed close by and to a man they rushed to the broken doorway and with one voice exclaimed, 'Where did that one go to?' Bairnsfather turned the situation into a cartoon of that title. It was an action that was to lead to a lifetime career built around the immortal character 'Old Bill' that emerged from his cartoons, collectively called *Fragments from France*. [It is a story that we examine in our biography *In Search of the Better 'Ole, The Life, the Works and the Collectables of Bruce Bairnsfather*.]

On 13 December 2003 the authors unveiled a bronze plaque on the cottage wall to commemorate the birth of Bairnsfather's inspired creation and the seeds of his extraordinary career.

Bairnsfather also decided to try his hand at sniping, considered an 'officer's sport', and climbed onto the roof of another cottage. He had hardly done so when another German barrage began and he had to beat a hasty retreat, an experience that he turned into the cartoon, *They've evidently seen me*, which shows a startled soldier clinging to a chimney as a huge shell whistles by. That cartoon is on the plaque.

It was in this area that men participated in that curious phenomenon, 'The Christmas Truce' on 24/25 December 1914. The 1st Battalion the Warwickshire Regiment in Plugstreet Wood took part in the truce and 2nd Lt Bruce Bairnsfather, in his book, *Bullets and Billets* gives a full and *humourous* account of what happened. After singing and shouting 'a complete Boche figure suddenly appeared on the parapet and looked about itself. This complaint became infectious. It didn't take Our Bert long to be up on the skyline. This was the signal for more Boche anatomy to be

---

Extra Visit continued

disclosed and this was replied to by all our Alfs and Bills until in less time than it takes to tell, half a dozen or so of each of the belligerents were outside their trenches and advancing towards each other in no-man'sland. The last I saw of this little affair was a vision of one of my machine gunners, who was a bit of an amateur hairdresser in civil life, cutting the unnaturally long hair of a docile Boche who was patiently kneeling on the ground whilst the automatic clippers crept up the back of his neck'. The experience may well have led to one of his Fragments cartoons entitled Coiffure in the Trenches where a soldier (either Alf or Bert) is having his hair cut by Old Bill as a large shell sails by. Bill is saying 'Keep yer 'ead still or I'll 'ave yer blinkin' ear off'.

Sir John French reacted quickly to the news of the truce. Units that had participated were moved out of the lines and hostilities immediately recommenced. Christmas Day 1914 was not without its official pleasures, however. Every officer and soldier in the field was given two gifts. The King and Queen sent a postcard bearing pictures of themselves, the King in service dress, and on the reverse in a facsimile of the King's hand the message, 'With our best wishes for Christmas 1914. May God protect you and bring you home safe. Mary R. George R'. Princess Mary, following a tradition that Queen Victoria had begun in the Boer War, sent an embossed brass tin containing a mixture of cigarettes, pipe tobacco and chocolate together with a small folded card wishing the recipient a Happy Christmas.

Turn round and return to the main road, turn left and rejoin the main itinerary.

On the slope to the right is the site of the old Château de la Hutte on Hill 63 under which the British built large subterranean shelters. At one time it was planned to build the Ploegsteert Memorial here.

Continue downhill to the large memorial on the right. Stop.

• Ploegsteert Memorial/Berkshire CWGC Cemetery Extension and Hyde Park Corner CWGC Cemeteries/Last Post/43.4 miles/ 15 minutes/Map 1/39, 1/38/RWC/Lat & Long: 50.73772 2.88234

(See pic on title pages). Here, since 7 June 1999, the Last Post has been played on the first Friday of the month at 1900 hours by local buglers. The event is organised by the *Comité du Mémorial de Ploegsteert* Chairman Jean-Claude

Walle. Special ceremonies may be requested. Tel: + (0) 56 58 84 41. Fax: + (0) 56 58 75 34. Email: www.auberge@skynet.be

Guarded by two lions, one baring his teeth, the other looking benign, designed by Sir Gilbert Ledward (who was to do work in the World War II Reichswald Cemetery on the Dutch-German border) is the Berkshire Cemetery Extension which was begun in June 1916. The rotunda structure is the Ploegsteert Memorial to the Missing bearing the names of 11,447 officers and men from nearby battles for every year of the war and has its own registers, separate to those for the adjoining cemetery.

There are **three VCs** commemorated on it: **Sapper William Hackett** of 254th Tunnelling Coy, RE, for helping to rescue men entombed with him in a mine after an enemy explosion on 22/23 June 1916, at Givenchy, and who was killed four days later; **Pte James Mackenzie** of the 2nd Bn Scots Guards for on 19 December 1914, at Rouges Bancs, rescuing a severely wounded man under very heavy fire and who was killed later that day attempting the same act; **Capt Thomas Tannatt Pryce** of the 4th Bn Grenadier Guards for on 11/12 April 1918, at Vieux Berquin leading an attack on the village, beating off 4 counter-attacks and driving off a fifth with a bayonet charge, who was last seen, with only 17 men and no ammunition, leading another bayonet charge. The Report for the memorial shows the continuing work of the Commission. Several entries have been amended as men whose names are inscribed on the Memorial have been identified in cemeteries, e.g. **Serjt J. B. Coutts**, now in Tournai Cemetery, and **Pte T. Gordie** buried in Le Grand Beaumont British Cemetery.

The Memorial was originally planned to stand in Lille, but the French were becoming 'disquieted by the number and scale of the Memorials which the Commission proposed to erect'. When the number of Imperial Memorials in France was reduced from the planned twelve to four (Soissons, La Ferté, Neuve-Chapelle and the Somme) extra land was acquired from the Belgians here at Ploegsteert. The names of the missing destined to be inscribed on other cancelled memorials were inscribed on memorial walls built inside the land assigned to a cemetery, e.g. Vis-en-Artois and Pozières. The disappointed architects of the aborted memorials were given other assignments. Thus Charlton Bradshaw, who had won competitions for his designs for Lille and Cambrai (another memorial which was cancelled) was allotted Ploegsteert and Louverval. This explains why the Memorial commemorates the Missing of the Battles of Armentières, 1914, Aubers Ridge, Loos and Fromelles, 1915, Estaires, 1916 and Hazebrouck, Scherpenberg and Outtersteene, 1918. It was inaugurated on 7 June 1931, by the Duke of Brabant, later to become King Leopold III. In 1981 a ceremony was held at the Memorial to celebrate the 50th anniversary of the inauguration. It was attended by Winston Churchill, grandson of Sir Winston Churchill, who died on 2 March 2010. His illustrious grandfather had served with the Royal Scots Fusiliers in the Ploegsteert sector after the humiliating end to the imaginative concept of the Dardanelles campaign, from 26 January to 3 May 1916.

[N.B. A **Plaque, showing Churchill** in his WW2 attire of Homburg hat and large cigar, can be seen on the wall of the Ploegsteert Town Hall, some .8 mile further on.]

In the cemetery are 295 UK, 51 Australian, 3 Canadian and 45 New Zealand burials, among them Anthony Eden's **Platoon Sergeant, 'Reg' Park** and Axel Alexander Olin whose nephew is buried in Messines Ridge Cemetery (qv).

Over the road is **Hyde Park Corner CWGC Cemetery** which was begun during Second Ypres by the 1st/4th Royal Berkshires, remained in use until November 1917 and contains the grave of **16-year-old Pte Albert Edward French,** the subject of a BBC Radio 4 documentary in 1983. He was killed on 15 June 1916, a week before his seventeenth birthday. Apparently the War Office refused the family a war pension as Albert had lied about his age on joining up and was under the official enlistment age when he was killed. The local Member of Parliament took up the case and eventually Albert's father received 5 shillings a week. His brother George spoke the words that gave the title to the radio programme about Albert, *He shouldn't have been there, should he?*

There are **Cafés** on either side of the road: beside the Memorial is the brasserie-style **Café des Touristes**. Tel: + (0) 56 55 60 66 and on the other side of the road is **l'Auberge**, HQ of The Last Post. Owned by Claude & Nellie Verhaege. Many WW1 souvenirs and artefacts. Closed Wed. Tel: (0)56 58 84 41. E-mail: restaurant@auberge-ploegsteert.be

In this vicinity the Commune of Comines-Warneton are planning an important WW1 Information Centre. They have already installed excellent Information Panels at points of interest in the area. These are described in a leaflet available from the Ploegsteert Tourist Office.

Turn, return to Ieper and the Menin Gate.

• *The Last Post Ceremony, Menin Gate/Model for the Blind/52.3 miles/20 minutes/Map 1/3/Lat & Long: 50.85217 2.89166*

This is where the echoes still remain, under the Menin Gate at 2000 hours every evening when the call of the Last Post rings out under the impressive arch. Just before 2000 hours two policemen arrive, stop the traffic and stand guard at each end of the gate. The buglers, just two in civilian clothes on most nights, or as many as six in uniform on special occasions, stand at the side of the road by the north-east pillar and, as the Cloth Hall clock strikes eight, they march together into the centre of the road, face the town and play the Last Post.

It is the very simplicity of the occasion that makes it poignant, the absence of martial organisation. Here are people gathered together in an orderly and respectful manner to remember, not because they have been told to do so but because they wish to do so. Now and again a particular regiment may bring a colour party to the occasion, a Legion branch or school cadet force may come, and so the ceremony may be extended by the laying of wreaths, the recitation of Binyon's words of Exhortation, the playing of the Reveille. There are, too, the growing number of conducted battlefield tours groups, but each bows to the Gate's tradition. This is not a ceremony extolling the glories of war. This is remembrance, acknowledgement of a debt by those that remain to those who sacrificed, together with the hope that knowledge of war's legacies might increase the chance of future peace. In our view it is not appropriate to applaud. When the ceremony is over, do thank the buglers. They are dedicated people

A British Fire Brigade Band parades under the Menin Gate.

from the local fire brigades and, often, Commonwealth War Graves gardeners. They take it in turns to play the nightly ceremony and they are proud and long-serving. Daniel Demey had been playing for well over fifty years and two others – Antoon Verschoot and Albert Verkouter – are not far behind. The twins, Rik and Dirk Vandekerchkove, are so alike that we joke they cannot tell each other apart. The ceremonies are co-ordinated by the Last Post Association, whose dedicated Chairman for many years was Mr Guy Gruwez, OBE (now Hon Chairman, the present Chairman is Benoit Mottrie), and the idea for the ceremony was that of Pierre Vandenbroembussche, Commissioner of Police in 1927. From 1 May 1929 the Last Post was sounded every day until interrupted by the Second World War, when the ceremony was continued at Brookwood cemetery near Pirbright. Twenty-four hours after the liberation of Ypres in September 1944 by the Poles the ceremony recommenced. On 8 October 1960 the Last Post was played for the 10,000th time. On 12 July 1992, the 75th Anniversary year of the Battle of Passchendaele, the 65th anniversary of the Menin Gate, was celebrated once more by the presentation of new bugles. On 31 October 2001, it was played for the 25,000th time. **Contact:** Tel: + (0) 57 48 66 10 Website: www.lastpost.be The website gives the daily number of times the Last Post has been sounded.

Walk up the steps on the left hand side (facing the Cloth Hall). At the top is

Model of the Menin Gate
This 1.9m long, 1.05m wide bronze model stands on a socle of Portland Stone and has a Braille text in 4 languages. It was cast by Dirk de Groeve and funded by the local Kiwanis Club (who also sponsored the Cloth Hall model in the Grand' Place). It was unveiled on 20 September 2003 by the blind Belgian singer, Séverine Doré.

• End of 1st, 2nd & 3rd Ypres Battlefield Tour

ALLIED AND GERMAN WAR GRAVES & COMMEMORATIVE ASSOCIATIONS

THE AMERICAN BATTLE MONUMENTS COMMISSION (ABMC)

'Time will not dim the glory of their deeds.' Gen John J. Pershing

The Commission was established by Congress in March 1923 and has been responsible for commemorating members of the American Armed Forces where they have served overseas since 6 April 1917 (the date of the US entry into WW1). Its task was to erect suitable memorials and cemeteries. It now administers 24 permanent burial grounds (in which there are 30,921 WW1 burials, in 8 cemeteries, of a total of 116,516 killed in the war), 21 separate monuments and three 'markers', as well as 4 memorials in the USA.

Memorial Day programmes are held on different days near to the actual Memorial Day on the last Monday in May in each ABMC Cemetery. Then each grave is decorated with the flag of the United States and that of the host nation (who donated the ground for the cemetery). There are speakers, usually including the appropriate American Ambassador, and the laying of wreaths with ceremonies that include military bands and units.

The American dead of the Salient are buried in Flanders Field Cemetery at Waregem (off the A19 motorway, direction Kortrijk). It contains 368 burials, the majority being of the 37th and 91st Divisions, 21 of which are unknown. Here is buried **Lt Kenneth MacLeish**, USNR, 15 October 1915, brother of the American Pulitzer Prize-winnning poet, social critic and educator, Archibald MacLeish.

Tel: + (0) 56 60 11 22. **USBMC** website where individual names can be searched: www.abmc.gov **Head Office:** Courthouse Plaza II, Suite 500, 2300 Clarendon Boulevard, Arlington, VA22201, USA. Tel: 001 703 696 6897. Fax: + 703 696 6666. Website: www.abmc.gov. **European Office:** 68 rue du 19 janvier, 92380 Garches, France. Tel: 00 33 (0)1 47 01 19 76. Fax: 0033 (0)1 47 41 19 79.

AMERICAN WAR MEMORIALS OVERSEAS INC

Non-profit organisation whose mission is to document, raise awareness of and care for private American gravesites and memorials where the US Government has no responsibility, liaising with local, national and international organisations.
Contact: Lil Pfluke. 6 rue du Commandant de Larienty 92210, St Cloud. Tel: 00 33 (0)6 1173 1332 E-mail: info@uswarmemorials.org Website: www.uswarmemorials.org

AUSTRALIAN WAR GRAVES

These are generally maintained by the CWGC. Nominal rolls of the war dead are held by the Dept of Veterans' Affairs. **Contact:** GeneralEnquiries@dva.gov.au

BELGIAN WAR GRAVES

Since 2004 the Belgian war graves have been administered by the Belgian Army. The nearest Belgian Military Cemetery to Ieper is in the Forest of Houthulst, (to the north of Poelkapelle on the N301) with 1,726 Belgian and 81 Italian burials. There is also a Belgian Military Cemetery at Westvleteren (1208 Belgian, 1 CWGC). From the road which passes Westvleteren church in the direction of Poperinge is a sign *'Militaire Begraafplats'* leading to the cemetery up a narrow road. This concentration cemetery contains 1,100 graves. Other Belgian Military Cemeteries are at Keiem, to the north of Diksmuide, with 628 burials, and Ramskapelle near Nieuwpoort, with 626 graves, 400 of which are unknown. There are two data bases for the Belgian 32,000 named and 10,000 missing dead of WW1 – one 'official' and one 'unofficial', not yet completed. **Contact:** Didier Pontzeele, Belgian War Graves, Institute for Veterans, Regentlaan 45-46, Brussels, Belgium. Tel: + (0) 2 227 63 34. Mobile: + (0) 47270224. E-mail: didier.pontzeele@lv-niooo.be

CANADIAN VIRTUAL WAR MEMORIAL

This searchable database contains information about the more than 116,000 Canadians and Newfoundlanders who have lost their lives since 1884 in major conflicts. **Contact:** www.virtualmemorial.gc.ca Also www.mapleleaflegacy.ca. **Contact**: Steve Douglas, c/o British Grenadier. E-mail: fa516600@skynet.be

COMMONWEALTH WAR GRAVES COMMISSION (CWGC)
'Their name liveth for ever-more' Ecclesiasticus 44.14

The full story of the Commission's founding (as the Imperial War Graves Commission) in 1917 by the then Major Fabian Ware and its subsequent history is told in our main Ypres-Passchendaele Guide.

Now the Commission's own comprehensive and informative **Website:** www.cwgc.org tells the on-going story in full, lists all the magnificent publications (e.g. Information Sheets on the *Battles & Memorials of the Ypres Salient, War Poets, Horticulture, Fabian Ware* etc), films and educational programmes they produce. It also offers a superb facility through its Debt of Honour roll of being able to search for the burial or memorial site of all the nearly 1.7 million servicemen and women of both world Wars it commemorates. One can also search by Cemetery to find a brief history and plan and list of those buried within.

The commission's beautifully-produced Annual Report, with its excellent coloured illustrations, is a mine of information about the never-ending maintenance work it continually undertakes. Now, approaching 100 years since the end of the Great War, masonry is beginning to crumble in a daunting number of cemeteries and a major programme of refurbishment is underway. Vandalism is another unfortunate headache. The annual budget runs at some £45 million.

Head Office: Commonwealth War Graves Commission, 2 Marlow Road, Maidenhead, Berks SL6 7DX , UK. Tel: 0044 (0) 1628 634221. Fax: 0044 (0) 1628 771208. E-mail Casualty & Cemetery Enquiries: casualty.enq@cwgc.org.

Area Office in Northern Europe: Elverdingsestraat 82, B-8900 Ieper, Belgium. Tel: + (0) 57 22 36 36. Fax: + (0) 57 21 80 14. E-mail: neaoffice@cwgc.org

JOINT CASUALTY & COMPASSIONATE CENTRE

In April 2005 the Army, Navy and RAF amalgamated in the JC & CC based at RAF Innsworth, part of the Service Personnel and Veterans' Agency, to deal with any remains of service personnel (principally from WW1 and WW2) that are found. This Agency replaced the MOD PS4(A) Compassionate Cell. They liaise with local embassies and the CWGC when remains are discovered and, if there is sufficient evidence with the remains to give hope of an identification, they then study historical case files etc. Once an identification has been made they use the media to trace any family, whose wishes regarding the form of reburial are then paramount. DNA

Tyne Cot Cemetery Memorial Wall and Headstones.

Entrance Gate, Tyne Cot Cemetery.

The Menin Gate, Ieper.

matching, for so long avoided by the Commission has now been undertaken for new discoveries, led by the Australians and Canadians. It was a major factor in the widely publicised identifications of some of the remains found in the mass grave discovered at Fromelles in 2008 (see www.cwgc.org/fromelles/). **Contact:** Sue Raftree, Tel: 0044 (0) 1452 712612, ext 6303. E-mail: historicso3.jccc @innsworth.afpaa.mod.uk. Website: www.mod.uk

FRENCH MINISTERE DES ANCIENS COMBATTANTS ET VICTIMES DE GUERRE

On 29 December 1915 a law was passed to guarantee a perpetual grave at State expense to every Frenchman or ally 'mort pour la France'. **Head Office:** 37 rue de Bellechasse, 75007 Paris 07 SP. Tel: 0033 (0)1 48 76 11 35. Website: http://www.cheminsdememoire.gouv.fr

VOLKSBUND DEUTSCHE KREIGSGRÄBERFÜRSORGE (VDK)

The German War Graves Organisation provides a similar service to that of the ABMC and the CWGC in looking after the German war dead and in assisting relatives to find and, in many cases, visit the graves. In 1925 a treaty was signed between Germany and Belgium to organise care of the German dead from the Great War.

Contact: *Volksbund Deutsche Kriegsgräberfürsorge,* Werner Hilperstrasse 2, D-34117 Kassel, Germany.

Belgian Office: Col Yvan Vandenbosch, Zwanebloemlaan 36, 2900 Shoten, Belgium. Tel: + (0) 36 46 08 75. E-mail: yvan.vandenbosch@skynet.be

WAR HERITAGE ALL-PARTY PARLIAMENTARY GROUP (WHAPG)

Consisting of members from both houses the group exists to support the work of the CWGC, to further educational programmes aimed at increasing knowledge of war heritage and battlefield sites, to support campaigners seeking to conserve and promote heritage sites and to encourage best practice in multi-disciplinary battlefield archaeology. It was formed in 2001 as a result of the threat posed to the Pilckem Ridge in the Ypres Salient by plans to extend the A19 motorway and is now concerned with battlefield sites in the UK and world-wide. **Chairman:** Lord Faulkner of Worcester. **Contact:** Joint Secretaries: Peter Barton (e-mail: pb@parapet.demon.co.uk, 8 Egbert Road, Faversham, Kent DE13 8SJ) and Peter Doyle (e-mail: doyle.towers@virgin.net) Website: www.wargravesheritage.org.uk

ARCHAEOLOGY IN THE SALIENT

There are two official departments:

1. Archeo7, led by archaeologist **Jan Decorte** (Reningelststraat 13, 8956 Kemmel, +32 (0)57 48 78 92 or +32 (0)473 46 01 78), archeologie@co7.be, www.archeo7.be is the (intercommunal) archaeological department of the towns of Ieper, Poperinge, Langemark-Poelkapelle, Zonnebeke, Heuvelland, Mesen and Vleteren. They are the ones that should be contacted first: any finds should be reported to them and they are allowed to give permission to others to dig within the 7 aforementioned municipalities.

2. VIOE West-Flanders, led by archaeologist **Marc Dewilde** ('De Blankaart', Iepersesteenweg 56, 8600 Diksmuide, Tel. +32 477 56 04 23 or +32 51 61 01 61, marc.dewilde@lin.vlaanderen.be) is the official body within the Flemish government, deals with all WW archaeology in the whole province.

Other important underground archaeology has been done by:

i. Association for Battlefield Archaeology in Flanders (ABAF) A scientific Association of historians, archaeologists and technicians founded in 1999 to research, survey, chart and preserve the pillboxes, bunkers and underground remains of WW1 in the Ypres Salient (e.g. Cryer Farm, Bayernwald, Letternberg etc). **Contact:** President and author **Franky Bostyn**, Tel: + (0) 51 77 04 41 (see also Passchendaele Memorial Museum).

ii. Joint authors of *Beneath Flanders Fields* and co-workers on 'Vampire' and other projects **Peter Barton** (see WHAPG above) and **Johan Vandewalle**, De Dreve Café, Polygon Wood, Tel: + (0)57 46 62 35 E-mail: johanvandewalle531@hotmail.com www.polygonwood.com

iii. The Diggers (qv),, amateur group who discovered Yorkshire Trench (qv), now disbanded.

Association des Musées et Sites de la Grande Guerre

A grouping of museums and preserved sites of the Western Front from Ieper in the north to the Vosges in the south-east. The VDK, CWGC, AMBC and WFA are associates. The aim is to preserve and promote international sites of the '14-'18 War. **Contact:** Secretary c/o Historial, B.P. 63 – 8201 Péronne Cedex. Tel: + 0033 (0)3 22 83 14 18. E-mail: df17@Historial.org,

Friends of In Flanders Fields Museum. Contact for information re subscriptions etc, Documentation Centre - see below.

Friends of St George's Church. Contact the Hon Sec: Mr K.A.E. Sears, 41 Winstanley Road, Sheerness, Kent, ME12 2PW.

Guild of Battlefield Guides

Launched on 28 November 2003 the Guild aims to provide a 'kite-mark' for Battlefield Guides. Patron: Prof Richard Holmes. The authors are Hon Members. **Contact:** Guild Secretary. E-mail: secretary@battleguides.org Website: www.battleguides.org

In Flanders Fields Documentation Centre. Contact: Dominiek Dendooven. **Open** Wednesdays from 0800-1200 and 1300-1700 or by appointment. Tel: + (0) 57 23 94 50. Fax: + (0) 57 23 94 59. E-mail: Stedelijke.Musea@ieper.be **Note** that this will be moving into the Cloth Hall by 2012. This will give more room to house and access its superb collection of books and ephemera and to pursue its major project of making data bases logging all the Belgian, French and German dead and missing of the Belgian WW1 Front.

The coveted and respected Badge of an accredited Guide of the Guild of Battlefield Guides.

Royal British Legion (RBL) Contact: Pilgrimage Dept., Aylesford, Kent ME20 7NX, UK. Tel: + (0) 1622 716729. E-mail: poppytravel@britishlegion.org.uk Website: www.poppytravel.org.uk

National HQ, 48 Pall Mall, London W1Y 5JY. **Ypres Branch: Contact:** Secretary: John Sutherland. Tel: + (0) 57 36 51 52. e-mail: john.hamilton@telenet.be

Ross Bastiaan Commemorative Plaques Contact: Website: www.plaques.satlink.com.au

Souvenir Français **Head Office:** 9 rue de Clichy, 75009 Paris. **Website:** www.souvenir-francais.com

Western Front Association (WFA) Contact: Hon Sec Stephen Oram, Spindleberry, Marlow Road, Bourne End, SL8 5NL Website: www.westernfrontassociation.com

TOURIST INFORMATION

Tourist Offices, Hotels & Restaurants are listed in a distinctive typeface.

I t is the ironic fate of a guide book that some information given in it will inevitably become out of date as soon as it is published. For instance, and perhaps somewhat surprisingly as we approach the centenary of the Armistice of 11 November 1918, new memorials are still being erected on the battlefields. Established ones are often dramatically altered by new landscaping by the Commonwealth War Graves Commission or to make way for new motorways, industrial estates or roundabouts which have completely altered navigation across the battlefields of Belgium over the past quarter century.

Hotels, restaurants and museums come and go or change hands and identity. New monuments are erected, old ones are refurbished, new historic sites are made safe to visit...

The information and advice we give here will mostly be of a general, rather than a particular, nature – with the exception of a few favourite haunts we cannot resist mentioning which are conveniently sited close to the battlefield and are sometimes mentioned in the actual itineraries rather than in the section below. But please do not blame us if you should be faced with the dreaded 'Under New Management' sign.

The very best advice is to go carefully through the itineraries that you intend to follow in this book, then **contact the appropriate national Tourist Offices at home at least one month before you leave**. List all the major towns you intend to visit, and request the following information, with relevant brochures (tourist literature is now of a generally high and helpful standard):

1. Addresses and phone numbers of local tourist offices with likely opening times. In smaller towns or villages these can be erratic, and we have found that whatever the information you may be given about them, the optimum time for getting in is 1000-1200 and 1400-1600 during the summer time. The most reliable and helpful offices in the battlefields areas are listed under their towns below

2. Listings of local hotels, bed-and-breakfast homes, self-catering lets, restaurants, museums, camping sites, etc, also maps and town plans. Staff are often discouraged from giving personal recommendations, but you can smile and try.

3. Specific information about battlefield routes for car drivers, cyclists and walkers. In the Salient there are well-marked circuits of different lengths, for motor driven, bicycle and pedestrian tourists, signed 'In Flanders Fields' Route, which use a standard rusty brown sign with cut-out poppy and Information Boards with photographs and historical backgrounds.

4. General tourist information/local attractions/cultural events/festivals, etc. The serious student of the battles may well wish to avoid the latter – the area will be congested, local hostelries full.

TELEPHONING BELGIUM/FRANCE/UK/USA
FROM ABROAD

Note: When phoning Belgium from abroad use the following prefix: 0032, indicated by '+' in the phone numbers listed in this guide, then drop the first local '0'. For France the prefix is 0033, for the UK 0044 and for the USA 001.

FLANDERS TOURIST OFFICES

Visit the website: www.visitflanders.com for the office appropriate to your home country.

They produce some attractive and helpful booklets – but not one composite one like the French – with details of how to get to Belgium, on local museums and attractions – and hotels (a new list every year). Beware – the French and Belgian versions of place-names are very different. You can be driving through France heading for Lille and when you cross the border into Belgium it disappears from the signposts to be replaced with Rijsel. Other traps are: Ypres-Ieper; Anvers-Antwerpen; Courtai-Kortrijk; Tournai-Doornik; Warneton-Waasten. In Flanders the native tongue is Flemish - also referred to as Dutch. There are some minor differences between Flemish and Dutch (a bit like the English spoken in the UK and the English spoken in the USA). English is widely understood and spoken - with everyone prepared to give it a try!

West Flanders Provincial Tourist Office, Konig Albert 1 - laan 120, B-8200 Brugge. For matters which concern tourism, visits, tourist literature etc, **Contact:** Valérie Heyman, Tel: + (0) 51 51 93 43. E-mail: valerie.heyman@westtoer.be Website: www.toerismewesthoek.be (click 'English' in top right hand corner). For matters which concern restoration, preservation, improvement of historical sites, monuments and commemorative events, principally for the Westhoek area, **Contact:** Frederick Demeyere. Tel: + (0) 51 51 93 65. Email: frederik.demeyere@west-vlaanderen.be

A huge project, '*De Westhoek Oorlog en Vrede*' (*War and Peace in the Flanders Fields Country*) has been undertaken by local historians to make an inventory (which can be consulted on the website www.wo1.be) of all war sites and relics in the area. Themed battlefield driving, walking and cycling routes (with their own small sketch maps, and an informative booklet, *The Flanders Fields Country & The Great War*, available at local tourist offices) are produced which include areas of particular WW1 historic interest, e.g. The Bluff and the Palingbeek, the 'Pop' Route, ' Craters and Mines' etc.

The Wereldoorlog I in de Westhoek website: www.wo01.be an initiative supported by the Province of West Flanders, gives details of cemeteries, memorials and other preserved sites in the Province. **Contact**: Robert Missinne, Tel: + (0) 57 48 72 69. E-mail: wo1@westhoek.be /www.greatwar.be

LOCAL TOURIST/INFORMATION OFFICES/WHERE TO STAY & EAT

Ypres. The Ieper/Westhoek Tourist Office is handily situated in the Cloth Hall (Stadhuis), Grand Place, B-8900 Ieper. Tel: + (0) 57 23 92 20.

E-mail: toerisme@ieper.be The staff are very helpful; and they produce their own booklets of tourist information in English, which are very comprehensive. They also sell guidebooks, maps and souvenirs in an attractive and well-stocked boutique. There is a separate leaflet for hotels and restaurants. It is difficult to have a bad meal in the cafés and restaurants around the Grand Place, but if you choose an environment with starched tablecloths, gleaming cutlery and glass, it can take a long time.

Around the square are to be found the following: the three-star **Regina Hotel**, reopened under new ownership on 11 November 2002 with 20 refurbished bedrooms, and two restaurants (one of which is 'gourmet'). Tel: + (0) 57 21 88 88, Fax: + (0) 57 21 90 20. E-mail: info@hotelregina.be Nearest to the Cloth Hall is the **In't Klein Stadhuis**, Tel: + (0) 57 21 55 42 and next is **The Anker** restaurant where a fine meal can be had, Tel: + (0) 57 20 12 72, but allow plenty of time. **The Trompet** (which serves a superb mixed salad and chips), Tel: + (0) 57 20 02 42, is very convenient and popular, especially for lunch. The **Kolleblume** (Poppy) Tel: + (0) 57 21 90 90, and the **Café Central**, Tel: + (0) 57 20 17 60, are reasonably priced and serve snacks as well as full meals. The **Vivaldi** tearoom/restaurant has undergone a major enlargement and provides a mix of snacks and full meals, Tel: + (0) 57 21 75 21. **The Old Tom** (one-star, Tel + (0) 57 20 15 41) has some hotel beds. The refurbished **Sultan** (three-star, Tel + (0) 57 20 01 93) no longer has a restaurant.

The superb **Hostellerie St Nicolas** restaurant that used to be in Boterstraat has moved to 532 Veurnseweg, Elverdinge, Tel: + (0) 57 20 06 22.

Local specialities are on offer in most of these restaurants. There are several hundred varieties of beer to choose from to wash them down, from thick dark brown almost treacley black concoctions like that brewed by the Trappist monks to light (blonde) lagers or even raspberry flavoured! A few hundred grammes of the renowned Belgian hand-made chocolates – on sale in half a dozen or so outlets in the square – make a perfect end to a calorific spree. You must not leave Belgium without sampling some of their legendary *frites* – quite irresistible with mayonnaise. Mussels are very popular – especially for family treats at lunchtime on Sunday. Pepper steak is also a favourite and the pancakes are yummy, as are leek flans and chicken stew. In fact Belgian cuisine is very good indeed.

If really pressed for time, buy a carton of those crisp frites and a sausage from one of the frituur windows and eat them on the hoof. If you want the maximum time on the battlefields, then there is a choice of shops/supermarkets around the square, along Coomansstraat or Meninstraat to buy the makings of a picnic. Along Coomansstraat/A Vandenpeereboomplein is the **'t Ganzeke** (Goose) restaurant with a varied menu. Worth a visit to see the superb posters of Ypres from post-World War I to the 1950s. Tel: + (0) 57 20 00 09. Further along, if you want a change, is the Chinese Restaurant, **Shanghai City**: Tel: + (0) 57 20 06 52.

> *Continue past the Theatre (by which there is a Mié Tabé Peace Post) on your right opposite St George's Church to the right-hand corner of the square and continue along the small Boezingestraat and Veemarkt.*

Ahead is the four-star, **Hotel Ariane**, Tel: + (0) 57 21 82 18. Fax: + (0) 57 21 87 99. E-mail: info@ariane.be. It is within an easy stroll of the Menin Gate and the Grote Markt and the best quality hotel in Ieper for battlefield tourers. It has a superb restaurant and bar, terrace, and a warm welcome by owners Natasja and chef Johann and all the staff. In 2010 a spacious and attractive reception area with WW1 exhibits and book stall was added to the pleasant enclosed and outdoor terraces which extend the dining area. There is a large car park.

The **Novotel** group has a 122 bedroom modern three-star hotel in Sint-Jacobsstraat just off the Grote Markt and near the Menin Gate. It has underground parking, fitness room and sauna. Tel: + (0) 57 42 96 00. Fax: + (0) 57 42 96 01. E-mail: H3172@accor-hotels.com Also in Sint-Jacobsstraat is the elegant three star **Albion Hotel** in a converted Flemish renaissance building with 20 ensuite rooms. No restaurant but an attractive lounge where breakfast is served. Tel: + (0) 57 20 02 20. Fax: + (0) 57 20 02 15. E-mail: info@albionhotel.be Opposite the Novotel is **The Old Bill Pub** whose pub sign, a Bairnsfather cartoon, originally hung outside the **Regina Hotel** in whose cellar a pub and private club was opened on 8 March 1969. The distinguished historian Dr Caeneepeel made a speech about Bruce Bairnsfather and his links with the Salient on the occasion.

Agriculture thrives again in the fields around Ieper and there is a growing industrial estate in the northern suburbs (see the 'Diggers' entry). This is served by a modern hotel, the **Best Western Flanders Lodge** (formerly the Rabbit), Tel: + (0) 57 21 70 00. Fax: + (0) 57 21 94 74. E-mail: bw-ieper@skynet.be. It is built in wood like a Swiss Chalet, with thirty-nine rooms with en-suite bathrooms, jacuzzi, restaurant and attractive bar, which is also used by visitors to the battlefields. It has been completely remodelled.

In Poelkapelle, some 7 miles from Ieper, is **Varlet Farm** (the original farm was named by the British and taken by the Hood Bn of the RND in October 1917), rebuilt in 1920. This B & B is popular with Battlefield tourists who are warmly welcomed by owners Dirk and Charlotte Cardoen-Descamps, Wallemolenstraat 43, 8920 Poelkapelle. Tel/Fax: + (0) 51 77 78 59. E-mail: info@varletfarm.com

At 54 D'Hondestraat (off the Grote Markt and on the site of the Old Shell Hole) is the renovated **Ambrosia Hotel**, with 9 ensuite bedrooms, run by Vincent Vandelannoote and Wona Danik. B+b and bar. Tel: (0) 57 36 63 66. Website: www.ambrosiahotel.be On Meensestraat as you walk towards the Menin Gate is the Poppy Pizzeria and Steak-house on the right. Tel: + (0) 57 20 55 50.

The British Grenadier & Salient Tours

A well-stocked book and map shop with a battlefield resource centre and computer facilities for looking up burials. Website: mapleleaflegacy.ca (qv). 5 Meensestraat, Ieper. Tel/Fax: + (0) 57 21 46 57, e-mail: fa516609@skynet.be
Base for guided Salient Tours, e-mail: tours@salienttours.com

Over the Top Tours (OTT) and Bookshop

Run by André and Carol de Bruin. A well-stocked book, map and souvenir shop, the base for guided tours of the Salient at 41 Meensestraat. Tel: + (0) 57 42 43 20. E-mail: overthetoptoursshop@skynet.be

The New Shell Hole Military Bookshop
Run by Patrick Indevuyst at Neermarkt 6, (just off the Grote Markt, to the left beyond the Cloth Hall). Mobile: + (0) 472 477 554, e-mail: indevuystpatrik@hotmail.com who maintains an excellent stock of old books, postcards, ephemera and collectables.

'T Klein Rijsel
This is a welcoming pub for all battlefield tourists – they even stock 'Peace Beer' served in special peace pots. Behind it is the excellent **Ramparts War Museum** with life-like scenes of trench life and original artefacts. By the Lille Gate. **Open** 1030-2000 (closed Wed & Thurs). Tel: + (0) 57 20 02 36.

Throwing a cat from the top of the Cloth Hall.

BATTLEFIELD TOURS
Battlefield tourism is a vital part of the economy of West Flanders – with visits by the British still among the most prominent. See **West Flanders Provincial Tourist Office** entry above.

Guided Battlefield Tours
In addition to the tours by qualified guides offered by the Ieper Tourist Office there are some locally based commercial organisations which run reliable regular English-speaking tours e.g:

    1. **Flanders Battlefield Tours.** Tel: + (0) 57 36 04 60. Fax: + (0) 57 36 06 60. E-mail: info@ypres-fbt.be Guided by well-known Jacques Ryckebosch and Genevra Charsley

    2. **Salient Tours**. See British Grenadier entry above.

    3. **Over the Top Tours.** See OTT entry above.

    4. **Trench Map Tours**, run by ex-RMP Iain McHenry, Plumerlaan 89/2b, 8900 Ieper. Tel: + (0) 57 58 61 31. Mobile: + (0) 473 762 710. Email: tours@trenchmaptours.com Website: www.trenchmaptours.com/

IEPER TODAY.
Once more the Grote Markt has become the scene of a bustling market each Saturday morning and in 1994 it received a major facelift when it was repaved and trees were planted, thus restoring it more to its pre-1914 aspect, so superbly documented in the photographs of 'Anthony of Ypres'. Some extremely 'modern' fountains were constructed at the same time which contrast strongly with the otherwise medieval appearance of the square. Nearby in May 1995 the Kiwanis erected a small **bronze**

The new terrace at the Ariane Hotel, Ieper.

Steve Douglas at The British Grenadier.

'Tubby Clayton', Talbot House.

'In Flanders Fields the Poppies Blow.'

Model of the Cloth Hall with raised features so that blind people can experience its shape.

There is also a series of interesting events to attract the visitor throughout the year. The Flemish have a capacity for enjoyment of their festivals and fairs which belies their somewhat dour image and these events are fun to attend. The medieval custom of throwing live cats from the Cloth Hall Belfry (the symbolic killing of evil spirits as personified by the cat) has been revived – with toy cats – in the Festival of the Cats, a colourful and popular carnival which takes place on the second Sunday in May every third year (next in 2012). Other regular events are the 100 Kilometres Ieper March on the weekend after Ascension, the 24 Hours Ieper Automobile Rally on the last weekend in June, the Thuyndag Fair, on the first Saturday and Sunday of August, the four days of the Ijzer March in mid-August, the Tooghedagen Craft and Antiques Fair on the second weekend in September and The Procession of St Martin on 10 November. Armistice Day is always celebrated on 11 November, whatever day of the week it falls on (not the nearest Sunday as happens now in Britain) and it is a public holiday. On that day there is a Belgian Memorial Service in St Martin's Cathedral and an English one in St George's Church, a 'Poppy Parade' and special ceremony at the Menin Gate. Hundreds of pilgrims come from the UK for this event and it is as well to apply early for tickets in the church – usually there is a 'spillover' service in the Cloth Hall with TV relay. This commemorates the sacrifice of all those who fought and, in particular, those who gave their lives, many willing and proud volunteers, in the Great War in Flanders.

Comines-Warneton Tourist Office. Chemin du Moulin Soete 21, B-7780 Comines. Tel: + (0) 56 55 56 00. E-mail: office.tourisme.comines-warneton@belgacom.net. Website: www.villedecomines-warneton.be

Heuvelland. Tourist Office 'De Bergen', 11 Reningelstraat, Kemmel. Tel: + (0) 57 45 04 55. Fax: + (0) 57 44 89 99. E-mail: <u>toerisme@heuvelland.be</u> They produce a Heuvelland booklet with walking and cycling routes, tourist info about events, lists of hotels, restaurant, camping sites etc. Very helpful.

Langemark-Poelkapelle Tourist Office, Kasteelstraaat 1, Langemark. Tel: + (0)57 49 09 41. e-mail: toerisme@langemark-poelkapelle.be

Mesen/Messines Tourist Information: Stadhuis, Markt 1, Mesen. Tel: + (0) 57 44 50 41. E-mail: toerisme@mesen.be

Messines Peace Hostel – 32 four-bedded studio-type rooms, restaurant, games room, facilities for the disabled. A 'Peace Project' by Vlaanderen Tourism, Mesen Council and N Ireland Maydown Ebrington Group. Tel: + (0) 57 22 60 40. E-mail: info@peacevillage.be Website: <u>www.peacevillage.be</u>

Poperinge. Tourist Office, Stadhuis, B-8970 Poperinge. Tel: + (0) 57 33 40 81, E-mail: tourisme@<u>poperinge.be</u> The annual Hop Festival is in September, and there is a signed, 54km 'Hop Route' around the area. Market day is on Friday (as it has been since the Count of Flanders granted permission for a market in 1187). They produce a leaflet called *Poperinge in the First World War* as well as the POP. Route booklet (for which there is a fee).

Accommodation etc:
Talbot House (qv), 43 Gasthuisstraat. Self-catering, clean and simple accommodation in this marvellously evocative setting. Tel: + (0) 57 33 32 28. E-mail: info@talbothouse.be **Hotel Amphora**, 3-star, attractive décor, 36 Market Square. Tel: + (0) 57 33 94 05. **Hotel Belfort**, 3-star, good restaurant, Market Square. Tel: + (0) 57 33 88 88. **Hotel Palace**, 3-star, good restaurant, 34 Ieperstraat. Tel: + (0) 57 33 30 93. **Hotel Recour,** Luxe, gourmet **restaurant Pegasus**, 7 Guido Gezellestraat. Tel: + (0) 57 33 57 25. There are several good restaurants and cafés around the main square which are convenient for a lunch break, e.g. the old WW1 favourite at No 16, the **De Ranke**, Tel: + (0) 57 33 30 08.

Vlamertinge
Hosts Liz and Jon Millward run the welcoming **Cherry Blossom b+b** (evening meals and guided tours on request). Grote Branderstraat 30, 8908 Vlamertinge. Tel: + (0) 57 30 15 55/+ (0) 47 23 47 694. E-mail: liz@cherryblossom.be

Zonnebeke. Tourist Office, Zonnebeke, Ieperstraat 7A, 8980 Zonnebeke.
Tel + (0) 51 77 04 41, Fax: + (0) 51 78 07 50, E-mail: toerisme@zonnebeke.be Website: www.zonnebeke.be. A new attraction is the Old Cheese Factory. This go-ahead commune has many sites of WW1 interest within its boundaries (e.g. Tyne Cot Cemetery, the new Memorial Museum, Letterberg Site, Kemmel, Zandvoorde etc) and often organises events with a WW1 interest, especially round the 11 November period.

ACKNOWLEDGEMENTS

During our 'recce and research' phase of this book we renewed many old friendships and made many new ones who were generous with their knowledge and their time.

As always we express our admiration for the dedicated work of the CWGC and for the assistance we have had from staff at Maidenhead and in Ieper. Frederik Demeyere, Co-ordinator *War & Peace in the Westhoek* gave us some very helpful information about future plans. In Ieper Piet Chielens Director of In Flanders Fields Museum, Fernand Vanrobaeys from the Tourist Office and Dominiek Dendooven from the Documentation Centre have been helpful as always. Natasja and the Staff of the Ariane Hotel looked after us extremely well during 'recces'. Chris Lock & Milena gave us info about the Tank Memorial. In Zonnebeke we have received much help from the enthusiastic Franky Bostyn. In Poperinge Annemie Morisse told us about the Lijssenthoek Project. We are grateful to Charles Hewitt and all the team at Pen & Sword Books for their on-going support, in particular, David Hemingway, our designer, for his extraordinary flexibility and unflappability.

PICTURE CREDITS

For the picture of the Menin Gate Buglers on the cover, the Tourist Office, Ieper and Last Post Committee; for the aerial photo of Tyne Cot Cemetery on page 54, Iain McHenry. For the portrait of Rupert Brooke on page 7, Charlotte Zeepvat.

INDEX
FORCES

These are listed in descending order of size, i.e. Armies, Corps, Divisions, Brigades, Regiments, then numerically and then alphabetically. Many more units are mentioned in the Cemetery descriptions throughout the book. 'Forces' listings include their Memorials.

MEMORIALS

MUSEUMS

WAR CEMETERIES

GENERAL INDEX